GOOD ENOUGH TO EAT

GOOD ENOUGH TO EAT

JEKKA McVICAR

With photographs by
DEREK ST ROMAINE

Kyle Cathie Limited

Distributed by
Trafalgar Square
North Pomfret, Vermont 05053

First published in Great Britain in 1997 by
Kyle Cathie Limited
20 Vauxhall Bridge Road, London SW1V 2SA

This edition published 1997

ISBN 1 85626 227 8

Photographs © Derek St Romaine
Photographs on pages 70, 71 and 119 © Jessica McVicar
Edible Garden Plans © Jessica McVicar and Saul Hughes
Book Design by Prue Bucknall
Printed and bound in Italy by Mondadori

Jessica McVicar is hereby identified as the author of this work in accordance with Section 77 of the Copyright, Designs and Patents Act 1988

A Cataloguing in Publication record for this title is available from the British Library

IMPORTANT NOTICE

This book contains information on a wide range of flowers. Before you cook or eat any flower or plant make sure you know whether or not it is edible. The reader is recommended to sample a small quantity first to establish whether there is any adverse or allergic reaction. Neither the author nor the publisher can be held responsible for any adverse reaction to the recipes, recommendations and instructions herein and the use of any plant, flower or derivative is entirely at the reader's own risk.

CONTENTS

ACKNOWLEDGEMENTS

With special thanks to Dawn for her inspired food styling, to Derek for his magnificent photographs, to Kyle for taking another gamble. Not forgetting Anthea for being on the end of a telephone and to Mac for his support and encouragement.

INTRODUCTION

The pride of every grove I chose,
The violet sweet and lily fair,
The dappled pink and blushing rose,
from **The Garland** by Matthew Prior
(1664-1721)

My inquisitive nature and habit of dead-heading plants as I walk around my herb farm has inspired me to write this book. It may seem eccentric and slightly hazardous to eat flowers; once you overcome the barrier of 'it's a flower' and not a herb or a vegetable, and you eat it for the first time, you will realise that it is not just a trendy thing, they really can be delicious. You will also discover that flowers have a unique flavour and texture and they can be a delicacy either on their own or when cooked with other ingredients.

History shows us that flowers have been eaten since records began. The Romans and Greeks used pinks and carnation petals in dishes. Orange blossom and pot marigold flowers have been used in Eastern cooking as far back as recorded history and are still used today. In China, lilies have always been eaten. Nasturtiums were well known and used by the ancient Persians in the fourth century BC. The Incas revered the sunflower and used it in ceremonies. Queen Elizabeth I, when unable to sleep, was said to have partaken of lavender tea as a mild sedative. It was not thought odd or quirky to add rose petals to dishes in Victorian times and

crystallised violets were considered a special delicacy.

I now look at flowers in a totally different light, not only admiring their beauty and scent, but also wondering what recipes I can use them in. When the coriander goes to flower it is time to start a second crop, the flowers can be used liberally and taste similar to the leaf (spicy, earthy, orangeish), with an extra hint of sweetness – lovely when added to salads, scattered over mushrooms or as a special garnish to a carrot soup.

In this book I will introduce you to some readily available flowers, with tips on how to grow them in your garden or in containers. I will also suggest recipes to try, some general ones such as the making of flower oils or vinegars, and some specific to

individual plants like Artichoke Hearts with Clover Flowers and Cucumber Sauce. It is amazing how the range of flavours, textures, shapes and colours of flowers will add a special something to the recipes. They will inspire any jaded palate and heart.

I do recommend that you take time to read the guide to edible flowers. This will offer you a few good hints about which parts of the flowers are the tastiest and which should be removed. I also provide a short list of flowers that you should most definitely avoid. If in doubt as to whether a flower is edible, err on the side of caution and do not eat it.

Amongst these Roses in a row,
Next place I pinks in plenty,
These double Pansies then for show;
And will not this be dainty?
from *Arrangement of a Bouquet* by
Michael Drayton (1563-1631)

Achillea millefolium
YARROW

❖

Perennial, Ht. 30-90cm (1-3ft). Small white flowers with a hint of pink, which grow in flat clusters from summer to autumn. It has been known in mild climates to be flowering at Christmas. The darkish green feathery leaves are highly aromatic and also edible in small amounts.

This ancient plant, steeped in magic and mystery, can be found growing wild in hedgerows. It has masses of flowers which have a vegetative flavour, mild and pleasant. They are great in salads and a true asset to many vegetable dishes. There are many hybrids such as *Achillea 'Taygetea'* and *Achillea clavennae*, which is a shorter variety. The flowers of these are all similar to *Achillea millefolium*, however only the petals are edible. They both can look most attractive in a border or container.

HOW TO GROW
SEED
Sow the small seeds in autumn in a prepared seed or plug tray. Cover the trays with cling film or glass and over-winter in a cold greenhouse or outside in a cold frame. Germination in spring can be erratic.

DIVISION
This is a more reliable way of propagation. Divide established plants in spring or early autumn.

WHERE TO PLANT
GARDEN
Choose the position in the garden with care. Yarrow survives by its creeping root stock, so place it in a position where you do not mind it spreading. It does not like growing in containers (see following section). If the soil is rich there will be a very enjoyable display; if the soil is poor the plants are likely to be a lot shorter. A compact plant will be formed, which can easily be used to fill in places you have difficulty in growing other plants. Yarrow is most accommodating and is very good in a dry corner of the garden as it is drought-tolerant.

CONTAINER
Yarrow does not grow happily in containers, although the hybrids such as *Achillea 'Taygetea'* and the shorter *Achillea clavennae* can look stunning. With both these hybrids eat the petals only. Cut back after flowering and keep watering to the minimum in winter.

WHEN TO HARVEST
Pick the flowers to use fresh as they appear. Preserve in oil or vinegar (see p142).

CULINARY
The whole flower of *Achillea millefolium*, the yarrow, can be eaten but do not forget to wash well before using. Divide the clusters, separating the individual flowers. I have found that too many whole flowers can be over-powering, so I use a maximum of five whole flowers and the petals from ten flowers as a general mix for a salad with a few yarrow leaves, which have been removed from their stalks.

WARNING
Yarrow leaves should only be eaten in small amounts, never more than three times a week. Large doses can produce headaches and vertigo. Picking the flowers can cause minor skin irritation. Medicinally it should not be taken by pregnant women.

YARROW, MUSHROOM AND BEANSPROUTS SALAD

Serves 4

5 whole yarrow flowers
Petals from 10 yarrow flowers
5 young yarrow leaves, finely chopped
350g (12oz) button mushrooms, sliced
100g (4oz) beansprouts, well washed
1 tablespoon olive oil
1 tablespoon lemon juice
1 clove of garlic, peeled and crushed

Prepare the yarrow flowers as mentioned above. Chop the yarrow leaves very finely, then mix them with the yarrow petals, mushrooms and beansprouts in a bowl. Whisk the oil, lemon juice and crushed garlic in a small container, pour over the salad and toss. Garnish with the whole yarrow flowers.

TOMATOES STUFFED WITH PINE NUTS AND YARROW FLOWERS AND PETALS

Serves 4

4 large tomatoes
15g (½oz) butter
1 tablespoon onion, finely chopped
75g (3oz) breadcrumbs
1 egg, beaten
2 tablespoons pine nuts
1 tablespoon yarrow petals
8 yarrow flowers

Sea salt and freshly ground black pepper to taste

Cut the tops off the tomatoes and hollow out the insides with a small teaspoon. Stand upside down to drain while you make the filling. Melt the butter in a saucepan, brown the onion gently and add the breadcrumbs and egg. As the mixture begins to thicken add the pine nuts and finally, when all is mixed together, season to taste. Leave to cool. When cool, stir in the yarrow petals. Put the mixture back into the tomato shells, place in a serving dish and sprinkle with the flowers. Serve as a starter or as a light main course with a green salad.

Agastache foeniculum
ANISE HYSSOP
❖

Perennial, Ht. 60cm (2ft). Long purple flower spikes in summer.
Aniseed-scented leaves.

This short-lived perennial herb is delightful to eat. It has blue/purple spikes, which flower throughout the summer, attracting bees and butterflies to the garden. The flowers, which have a very small amount of scent, have a sweeter aniseed taste than the leaves which are more commonly used in cooking. They combine well with green salads, vegetable dishes, pastas and fruit salads, fruit tarts and pavlovas. Other agastaches worth looking out for are *Agastache rugosa*, Korean mint, and *Agastache mexicana*, Mexican agastache. The flowers are very similar to anise hyssop in colour and shape. The flavour of the flower from both varieties is more a mixture of mint and aniseed.

HOW TO GROW
SEED
Thinly sow the small seed in spring under protection in a seed or plug tray. Keep at 18°C (65°F) to germinate.

CUTTINGS
These can be taken from the new

growth in late spring, or from semi-ripe cuttings in the late summer.

WHERE TO PLANT
GARDEN
This plant will adapt to most soils but, if given a choice, it prefers a rich, moist soil in full sun. Plant out in spring when the soil has started to warm and all threat of frost is gone.

CONTAINER
Anise hyssop does grow to about 60cm (2ft), but do not let this put you off, because it looks most attractive especially when placed in a collection of terracotta pots.

WHEN TO HARVEST
The flowers are best used fresh. This is no problem as the herb flowers for most of the summer, giving plenty of time to gather the flowers as they open. They can be pulled from the flowering spikes without having to remove the head and therefore destroying the look of the plant.

Preserve the flowers in oil, butter or vinegar (see p138). If you wish to dry the flowers, cut the whole flowering spike off including some length of stem. This will make it easier to dry (see p146). Use them in dried arrangements. The flower loses all flavour in drying so it would only be worth adding to culinary dishes for the colour.

CULINARY
Float the flowers in fruit salads and fruit cups, and sprinkle over mashed potato, glazed onions, glazed carrots and any marrow dish. They are also delicious added to pasta dishes just before serving.

RIGHT: mushroom ciabatta (see p17)

ANISE HYSSOP SALAD

Serves 4
½ iceberg lettuce, sliced
½ Chinese leaves, sliced
1 endive, sliced
1 teaspoon anise hyssop leaves, finely chopped
4 anise hyssop flowers, finely chopped
10 anise hyssop flowers removed from main spike, divided into individual segments
2 anise hyssop flowers and 8 leaves left whole for garnish

French dressing
3 tablespoons thyme olive oil (or plain olive oil)
1 tablespoon white wine vinegar
1 teaspoon French mustard
Salt and freshly ground black pepper

Mix the iceberg lettuce, Chinese leaves, endive and finely chopped anise hyssop leaves together. Toss in the flowers. Make the French dressing by mixing all the ingredients together, pour over the salad and then toss. Decorate the serving dish with the whole anise hyssop leaves, place the salad in the middle and decorate with the whole flowers. Serve.

COURGETTE AND ANISE HYSSOP FLOWERS

Serves 4
4 young courgettes
4 full flower spikes anise hyssop
6 anise hyssop leaves
4 tablespoons anise hyssop flowers

Vinaigrette
4 tablespoons olive oil
2 tablespoons tarragon vinegar
Salt and freshly ground black pepper

Wash the young courgettes and place them in a pan of boiling water for four minutes. Drain and cool. Cut them in half, scoop out the soft centre pulp and put on one side. Place the eight courgette shells onto a serving dish. Finely chop the leaves and mix them into the pulp and then add three tablespoons of flowers. Put the mixture into the shells, decorate with the four flower spikes and remaining flowers, and serve with the vinaigrette dressing.

MUSHROOM CIABATTA

Ciabatta is one of a range of delicious breads now widely available in supermarkets. The photograph on p15 shows ciabatta served with sautéed mushrooms and melted cheese and topped with anise hyssop flowers.

TIP
The seed heads look lovely in dried flower arrangements

Alcea rosea
HOLLYHOCKS

❖

Biennial, Ht. 1.2-2.5m (4-8ft). Spike of single hibiscus-like flowers in a range of colours from pink, yellow, cream and white from summer to early autumn. Rounded lobed, rough-textured green leaves.

These beautiful flowers once were so popular that they had their own special floral exhibition class. Now, alas, they have taken a back seat, but with so much nostalgia for the past and for cottage gardens, I hope they may come back into fashion. The flowers are delicious to eat, having a light floral flavour which changes in description from person to person, plant to plant!

HOW TO GROW

SEED
Sow the seed either in early autumn under protection in a cold greenhouse or in spring. A little bottom heat of 18°C (65°F) is beneficial to help germination.

DIVISION
Divide the plant after flowering by separating the crowns, leaving one or more buds in each clump and as many roots as possible on each piece.

CUTTINGS
Take cuttings of about 2.5cm (1in) in length from the side shoots of the old root at almost any time, potting them singly in a prepared pot or plug tray and keeping them shaded until the roots are formed. Do not over-water as the cuttings will rot.

WHERE TO PLANT

GARDEN
Plant in spring after the last frosts, at the back of a well-prepared border in full sun, adding compost if the soil is poor. Plant 60cm-1m (2-3ft) apart. The plants may need protection at first on cold nights, and plenty of water during the summer. A top dressing of compost manure is helpful when the flowering spikes appear. After flowering, the spikes should be cut down to about 15cm (6in) from the ground. If you experience winters that are both cold and wet I suggest that the mature roots are lifted in winter and stored in cold frames. However it may be easier to start again from cuttings or seed.

CONTAINER
Hollyhocks are too tall to be happily grown in containers.

WHEN TO HARVEST
Pick flowers when open, collect carefully and use immediately. Alternatively the flowers can be held over by cutting the stems with the flowers on and putting them in water. The flowers can then be carefully picked off and prepared just before serving.

CULINARY
Before eating remove the centre stamen and any green bits. Use fresh in salads. Hollyhocks can look stunning if crystallised (see p142) and used to decorate puddings from fruit fools to fruit salads. Hollyhocks also make a very subtle-flavoured syrup (see p141) which can be used with different puddings.

TIP
Beware of rust which may make the foliage shrivel and if left untreated may kill the plant. Remove and burn diseased leaves immediately. Do not plant anywhere near mint because the rust will spread.

Here are two very attractive salads, especially if made using hollyhocks of different colours.

HOLLYHOCK, ENDIVE, ORANGE AND WALNUT SALAD

Serves 4
2 endives, washed and torn apart
6 oranges
25g (1oz) walnuts, chopped
6 hollyhock flowers with their centre stamens removed
2 whole hollyhock flowers for garnish

Salad dressing
200ml (7fl oz) crème fraîche (low fat)
4 tablespoons olive oil (not extra virgin, as it is too strong a flavour)
2 tablespoons lemon juice
Freshly ground pepper and salt

Mix the endives with the grated rind of one orange in a serving bowl. Squeeze the juice from the orange that has had its rind removed and set aside. Remove all the peel and pith from the remaining five oranges and slice so you have rounds 5mm (¼in) thick, and add to the bowl. Finally add the walnuts, toss, cover and refrigerate until just before serving. Make the dressing by mixing the crème fraîche with the reserved orange juice; beat in the oil and gradually add the lemon juice and salt and pepper to taste. Pour the completed dressing over the endive, oranges and walnuts, toss. Add the flowers and gently toss, decorate with the whole flowers and serve.

HOLLYHOCK AND PEAR SALAD

Serves 4
4 pears, cored and cut into slices (peel if preferred but not necessary)
150ml (¼pint) pear or white grape juice
8 hollyhock flowers, with their centre stamens removed
4 whole hollyhock flowers for garnish

Put the sliced pears into the pear or grape juice, add the flowers, and toss. Put into a serving dish and decorate with the four whole flowers.

Allium schoenoprasum
CHIVES
❖

Perennial, Ht. 20cm (8in). Purple/pink flowers in spring. Leaves and flowers have a mild onion flavour.

This was the first flower that I ate many years ago. I was standing by the chives picking off the flowers to promote more leaf growth and, as they look similar to clover (if you screw up your eyes), I thought they might taste good. They certainly do – a crunchy, mild onion flavour. I have since added them to many dishes, from baked jacket potatoes to salads of every description. My favourite is bread sauce.

Some other varieties of Allium well worth looking out for are: the pink flowering chives, *Allium schoenoprasum roseum*, and the white flowering variety, *Allium schoenoprasum* 'White Form'. Both are good to eat, having the same flavour as the more common purple flower species. *Allium tuberosum*, garlic chives, is another story. It has attractive white star flowers, totally different from the chives mentioned. It is superb to eat. The flowers taste of sweet, crunchy garlic and give a substantial boost to many dishes especially salads when a more garlicky flavour is appropriate.

HOW TO GROW
SEED
Sow the black seed in spring under protection in a seed or plug tray. They need a heat of 19°C (65°F) to germinate. Alternatively wait until the soil has begun to warm up and sow directly into the garden in rows or clumps.

DIVISION
Divide the clumps every few years in spring and replant in the garden in groups of six to ten bulbs, at a distance of 15cm (6in) apart.

WHERE TO PLANT
GARDEN
Plant in a rich, moist soil in a fairly sunny position, in spring when all threat of frost has gone.

CONTAINER
They grow well in pots, if positioned in semi-shade and not in the full sun. Use a liquid feed in the flowering season.

WHEN TO HARVEST
Cut the flowers right off the plants (including the stem) when they are fully opened but before the colour fades. Chives start flowering on mature clumps in early spring and on young plants in late spring. The young plants can keep flowering well into summer if the weather is not too arid.

CULINARY
Apart from baked jacket potatoes, salads and bread sauce, the flowers can be used to decorate and flavour many dishes. The crunch enhances a tomato salad; it also adds a touch of the exotic when sprinkled over French beans before serving. Equally it looks most attractive in stuffed avocado.

BREAD SAUCE

I use this sauce with roast chicken and turkey. There are no chive flowers at Christmas-time, and unfortunately they do not freeze very well, so use for a Thanksgiving or a summer roast.

75g (3oz) breadcrumbs, stale white or brown, not granulated
450ml (¾pint) milk
1 small onion, peeled
¼ teaspoon grated nutmeg
8 whole cloves
5 chive flower heads

Well before you need the sauce, stick the cloves into the onion, add the milk and place in a small pan. Grate a small amount of nutmeg on the top and, over a gentle heat, bring to the boil. Remove from the heat, cover the pan and allow to stand and infuse for two hours or more. To make breadcrumbs use a processor or liquidizer. If the bread is truly stale it can be grated. When you are ready to make the sauce, remove the onion stuck with cloves, add the breadcrumbs and, over a very low heat, stir until the breadcrumbs are well mixed in and the sauce has thickened. This will take approximately ten minutes. Remove the pan from the heat, add the chive flowers and stir well. Put in a warmed dish and serve.

SOURED CREAM AND CHIVE FLOWER FILLING FOR BAKED JACKET POTATOES

This recipe can be used as a dip, with cauliflower, or any other vegetable dish where you would like the mix of chive, cream and vegetable.

142ml (5fl oz) soured cream
1 tablespoon chives, cut
6 chive flowers, broken up into individual florets
Some whole chive flowers for decoration

Cut the chives with scissors from the plant, then snip them into a small mixing bowl, add the soured cream and stir well. Add the chive florets and mix. Cover with cling film, and keep refrigerated until needed. Before serving, place the whole flowers around the bowl for decoration.

TIP
Plant chives next to roses to prevent black spot.

Aloysia triphylla
LEMON VERBENA

❖

Half-hardy, deciduous perennial, Ht. 1-3m (3-9ft). Tiny white flowers tinged with lilac in early summer through to early autumn. Lemon sorbet-scented and pointed lance-shaped, mid-green leaves.

This is the Rolls Royce of herbs. Anyone who has rubbed the leaves and smelt that sharp lemon scent can never forget it. Often I see people in gardens gently caressing the plant and then smelling their hands, pleasure showing in their faces. The flowers are small and delicate, growing in small pyramids. Their size really belies the flavour, a true lemon sorbet, which is the same as that of the leaves. They combine well with many fruit dishes, from strawberries and raspberries to melon, and are ideal in fruit salads.

HOW TO GROW

SEED

The seed sets only in warm climates. I have succeeded only once in England in the hot summer of 1995. Sow the small seeds thinly in spring, under protection in a seed or plug tray. A bottom heat of 15°C (60°F) helps germination.

CUTTINGS

These can be taken from the new growth in the late spring or from semi-ripe cuttings in the summer.

WHERE TO PLANT

GARDEN

This plant originates from a warm, humid climate so it needs protecting from frost, wind and temperatures below 4°C (40°F). The soil should be light, warm and free-draining. An ideal place is against a south-facing wall. Prune the plant in autumn and trim in spring to maintain shape.

CONTAINER

Lemon verbena is well suited to growing in containers, but it must be allowed to rest in winter and drop its leaves; so place the container in a warm, sunny, light spot and in winter, protect from frosts by placing the container in a cold greenhouse and allowing the compost nearly to dry out. Trim the plant to maintain shape in the spring and autumn.

WHEN TO HARVEST

Pick the flowers to use fresh when needed. They are so small that they do not store well. Pick the leaves any time before autumn. The leaves dry very quickly and easily and can be stored in a well-sealed container.

CULINARY

The flowers and leaves both combine well with drinks, fruit salads, jellies, cakes, stuffings, apple dishes and home-made ice cream.

TIP

If you are growing this plant in a conservatory or green house, look out for red spider mite. Once spotted treat immediately with liquid horticultural soap according to the manufacturer's instructions.

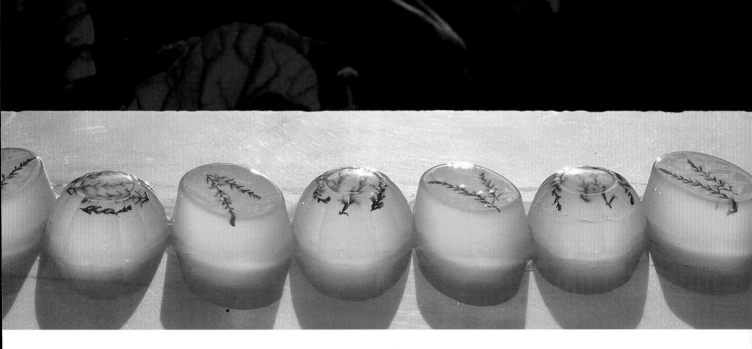

LEMON VERBENA AND CARROT SALAD

Serves 4
6 carrots, washed
2 tablespoons lemon verbena flowers
6 lemon verbena leaves, finely chopped
1 tablespoon pine nuts

Vinaigrette
3 tablespoons olive oil
1 tablespoon white wine vinegar
Salt and pepper to taste

Grate the carrots by hand or using a food processor. Mix with the lemon verbena flowers and leaves and the pine nuts. Make the vinaigrette by thoroughly mixing all the ingredients together. Pour over the carrots and lemon verbena. Toss well and serve.

LEMON VERBENA JELLY

Jelly is not difficult to make. It is so reminiscent of children's parties that it is often overlooked for a more sophisticated pudding.

Makes 8 small jellies
600ml (1 pint) water
10 lemon verbena leaves
1 sachet gelatine or, if you are vegetarian, 2 teaspoons agar powder
Juice of half a lemon
Caster sugar to taste
2 tablespoons fresh flowers of lemon verbena, plus a few more

Bring the water to the boil, put in the lemon verbena leaves and stir well. Cover, remove from heat and leave to infuse for ten minutes, strain and reheat to simmering point. Remove from the heat and sprinkle the gelatine or agar powder over the surface, stirring briskly until thoroughly mixed. Add the lemon juice, sugar to taste and 1½ tablespoons of flowers. Mix well and pour into a jelly mould or individual serving containers. Sprinkle the remaining flowers over the top. Chill in the refrigerator until set. If you wish to serve the jellies out of their moulds, dip them in warm water and then turn them out. Decorate with some more flowers and serve.

Anethum graveolens
DILL
❖

Annual, Ht. 60-150cm (2-5 ft). Tiny yellow/green flowers in clusters all summer. Fine aromatic green leaves.

This annual culinary herb is very well known for its leaves, which are used with gravlax, soused herrings and in marrow dishes. The seed not only combines well with vegetables, but is also effective medicinally as a mild antispasmodic. The flowers, on the other hand, have been overlooked. They have a slightly sweet dill-ish flavour with a hint of mint and combine well with vegetables, salads, potatoes and of course fish dishes. They are also lovely in vinaigrettes, mayonnaise and pickles. Another species well worth looking out for is fern leaf dill, *Anethum graveolens* 'Fernleaf', a more compact plant, and very good for leaf production. The flower is identical to *Anethum graveolens* and can be used in the same way.

HOW TO GROW
SEED
Sow the seed in spring under protection in a plug tray or pot. Do not use seed trays as dill hates having its roots disturbed when being transplanted. It will need heat to germinate, 19°C (65°F). Alternatively wait until late spring when the soil has begun to warm up and sow direct into the garden in shallow drills on a prepared site. Protect from frost and excessive rainfall. When large enough to handle, thin to a distance of 20cm (8in) apart. I recommend successive sowing throughout the season to maintain a good supply.

WHERE TO PLANT
GARDEN
Plant in a well-drained, poor soil in a very sunny position. Young plants can be a bit tender and may need supporting, so put sticks around to stop them toppling over. Also protect them from slugs.

CONTAINER
I am aware that some may think I am mad to suggest that dill can be grown in containers. However it is quite feasible if a large pot or trough is used and a number of seeds are sown directly into it. When large enough to handle thin to 6cm (2½in) apart, a lot closer than you would have plants in the garden. Keep cutting for leaf production but, if you want flowers, stake the plants to stop them falling over, harvesting the flowers when needed. I also suggest that, for a constant supply of leaves or flowers, a number of pots is kept going at different stages.

WHEN TO HARVEST
Pick the complete flower head when it is yellow all over. Separate the individual tiny flowers from the main head and use fresh or freeze (see p144). They will keep for a few days in the salad compartment of the refrigerator. Alternatively make dill flower vinegar or oil (see p142), both of which are very useful in the kitchen.

CULINARY
The individual flowers are minute but can be eaten whole. Add a whole flower head to pickled gherkins, cucumbers and cauliflower and it will give a flavour stronger than the leaf but milder and fresher than dill seed (see floral vinegars, p142).

TIP
When planting dill in the garden avoid siting it near fennel because you will corrupt the flavour of both herbs and land up with 'Fendill'.

DILL FLOWER TEA

Most people have heard of dill seed tea which is both refreshing and medicinal. So is the flower tea which, although similar, has a more delicate flavour. It is delicious served warm or cold as a refreshing summer drink, with an added slice of cucumber.

Makes 1 cup

2 complete flower heads, washed and placed in a tea pot or cup

Pour on boiling water, cover, and leave to infuse for five minutes. Strain and drink. You can add a small floral sprig of dill if you wish to decorate the drink.

SOUSED HERRING WITH DILL FLOWERS AND LIME

Serves 6

6 herrings, split and boned
6 peppercorns
2 blades of mace
2 allspice or myrtle berries
1 clove
1 bay leaf
1 onion, thinly sliced
½ teaspoon soft brown sugar (optional)
300ml (½ pint) dill vinegar (see p142)
Juice from one lime
150ml (¼ pint) water
Freshly ground sea salt
1 tablespoon dill leaves, chopped
2 tablespoons dill flowers, all greenery removed

1 lime, thinly sliced
Preheat oven to 160°C, 325°F, gas mark 3

Ask the fishmonger to split and bone the herrings. Roll the prepared fish from head to tail and pack them in a deep ovenproof dish or casserole. Put all the spices and the bay leaf into a pan with the onion, sugar (if using), dill vinegar, lime juice and the water. Add a pinch of salt and bring to the boil. Allow to cool, then pour over the herrings. The liquid should just cover them. Cook for one hour. Remove from oven, allow to cool, then cover and refrigerate. Before serving, scatter the dill leaves over the top, arrange the sliced lime and finally decorate with the flowers.

25

Angelica archangelica
ANGELICA
❖

Biennial or short-lived perennial, Ht. 1-2.5m (3-8ft). Highly scented green/white
flowers in the second year from spring until summer.
Bi- or tri-pinnate bright green leaves.

I will never forget the first time I really noticed the flower of angelica. I was
walking down to my farm and noticed this sweet scent wafting all around.
I tracked it down and found it was the angelica. The scent resembles an
aromatic cow parsley to which this plant is related. The small flowers taste
as good as they smell, combining well with salads, vegetable dishes, fruit
salads and fruit tarts. Another species of angelica really worth growing is
Angelica gigas which has stunning red flower heads in early autumn.

HOW TO GROW
SEED
The seed of this plant is very short-
lived, being viable for only about three
months. For the best crop, sow in
early autumn into a prepared seed
or plug tray or direct into a pot,
wintering the seedlings outside. For
seeds older than three months, place in
the freezer of your refrigerator for
four weeks before sowing.

WHERE TO PLANT
GARDEN
Angelica is a striking plant in its
second year so plant it at the back of a
border near a wall in a rich deep soil.
It dislikes hot, humid climates and is
much happier if it has some shade at
the height of the day. Plant out at a
distance of 1m (3ft) from other plants.

CONTAINER
Surprisingly, considering its size, this
is possible and I have first-hand
experience of growing angelicas in
containers for exhibition. The knack is
to keep potting the plant up into the
next size pot as it grows, minimising
any disturbance to the large tap root.
A warning sign to pot on is when
the plant needs a lot of watering.
Position the container in partial
shade and keep well watered. Stake
when necessary.

WHEN TO HARVEST
Pick the flower head in early spring
just as it opens fully and use it fresh or
preserved. One of the best methods of
preserving this flower is to make a
floral syrup (see p141). The flavour is
reminiscent of candied angelica.

CULINARY
Everyone is aware of candied angelica
being used to decorate cakes and
candies. The flowers have the same
sort of flavour but sweeter. They
combine well with cream cheese and
crème fraîche. I have used them with
lemon, lime and tangerine sorbets but
my most ambitious one was made from
the angelica stems and the flowers.
This took a little adjusting to get the
flavour right without blowing the top
off my taste buds!

WARNING
Wild angelica can be confused
with *Oenanthe crocata*, water
hemlock also known as water
dropwort, which is poisonous.
Equally this is one of the few
herbs to burn my skin. So take
care when cutting the plant down
or harvesting the stalks for use
in candying.

TIP
A tea made from the young leaves
is good for reducing tension and
nervous headaches.

ANGELICA SORBET

Serves 4

1 piece fresh, young angelica stem,
8-10cm (3-4in) long and cut into
small pieces
600ml (1 pint) water
250g (8oz) granulated sugar
3 tablespoons angelica flowers
Juice of half a lemon
1 tablespoon egg white, whisked
(optional)

Put the angelica stems, water, sugar and one tablespoon of angelica flowers together into a small pan and bring slowly to the boil, stirring from time to time to make sure the sugar dissolves and does not stick to the bottom. Simmer for approximately eight minutes or until the angelica stem sections are soft. Strain this liquid, add the lemon juice and check for sweetness. If too sour, add more sugar. Allow to cool before pouring into a freezing tray and putting in the freezer. Leave for ten minutes, then, using a whisk or fork, mash it up. Keep doing this until the mixture resembles a slush. Then mix well into the slush the tablespoon of egg white and a further tablespoon of flowers. At this point you can either return the mixture to the freezing tray or to individual serving dishes if you have room in your freezer. Take out of the freezer ten minutes or so before serving and decorate with the remaining tablespoon of flowers.

WILTED SALAD WITH ANGELICA FLOWERS

Serves 4

4 firm round lettuces
2 rashers middle back bacon
1 carrot
1 tablespoon angelica flowers, stalks removed
1 onion
300 ml (½ pint) well-flavoured chicken or vegetable stock
1 tablespoon parsley, chopped
Preheat oven to 180°C, 350°F, gas mark 4

Wash the lettuces and put them into a pan, cover with cold water and bring to the boil. Immediately remove from the heat, strain, and douse in cold water to revive. Shake and dry on kitchen towel.

Grease an oven-proof dish and line the bottom with rashers of bacon. Finely chop the carrot, most of the angelica flowers (reserving a few whole ones for the garnish) and the onion, and sprinkle over the bacon. Place the whole lettuces on top. Pour over the stock and cover. Cook in the oven for 45 minutes. Arrange the lettuces on a dish for serving. Reduce the stock in which they were cooked by two-thirds and pour over the lettuces. Sprinkle with the parsley and the remaining angelica flowers.

Borago officinalis
BORAGE

❖

Annual, Ht. 60cm (24in). Blue or purplish star-shaped flowers in early summer. Bristly oval leaves.

Borage is synonymous with Pimms No.1. The very attractive blue flowers are much more versatile. Their flavour is of mild cucumber, as are the leaves, and combines well with cream cheese, tomatoes and fruit and looks great in salads and fools. There is a white-flowered borage, *Borago officinalis* 'Alba' which is becoming more popular. This is just as good to cook with as the blue-flowered variety.

HOW TO GROW

SEED

Sow the seed in early spring under protection in a plug tray or pot. Try to avoid a seed tray because borage dislikes its roots being disturbed when transplanted. Plant out as soon as the danger of frost has passed at a distance of 60cm (24in) apart.

WHERE TO PLANT

GARDEN

Borage prefers a well-drained, light, poor soil of chalk or sand in a sunny position. It can be happily sown thinly direct into a prepared site as soon as all threat of frost has gone and the soil has started to warm.

CONTAINER

To grow borage successfully the container must be large. It is much more effective if grown with other plants, for example, when planted in the middle of a half beer barrel with other culinary herbs planted around it. This way the plant has room to grow, will not topple over, and looks very good as a centrepiece.

WHEN TO HARVEST

These flowers will freeze (see p144), so pick when they are just fully opened. The young leaves do not freeze or dry very successfully, therefore cut the leaves when they are young and use fresh.

CULINARY

The blue of the flowers looks great tossed in salads, crystallised on cakes (see p142) or added to iced summer soups. They are lovely with curd or cream cheese. To get the best taste it is important to remove the pistils and stamens of this flower before eating. These are very easily seen, comprising the whole of the black centre.

TIP

Borage is a good companion plant, which can be a plus and a minus. The plus is the attraction to bees, beneficial in pollinating other plants; for example, if you plant borage at the end of rows of runner beans this will increase the yield. The minus is borage's attraction to black fly so you may need to spray it off with a high-pressure hose before you can harvest.

BORAGE ICE CUBES

A tray for making ice cubes
As many borage flowers as are needed
to put one in each cube

Remove the centre stamen and pistils from the flowers and place one in each cube. Pour in sufficient water to fill the tray, place in the freezing compartment. When frozen, remove from the ice cube tray and use as required. The ice cubes look lovely in summer drinks or in fruit salads.

GOOSEBERRY AND BORAGE FLOWER FOOL

Because everyone's sugar requirements are different I have not specified how much to add. Equally the gooseberries can vary, some being so sweet that a minimal amount of sugar is needed.

Serves 4

450g (1lb) red or green gooseberries
Caster sugar to taste
200ml (7fl oz) crème fraîche
2 tablespoons borage flowers,
prepared
12 whole borage flowers

Cook the gooseberries in a large pan with two tablespoons of water and a small amount of sugar. Stir from time to time. When soft, turn off the heat and allow to cool in the saucepan. Check for sweetness, adding sugar if necessary. Put the gooseberries into a food processor or liquidizer and purée. Place the crème fraîche into a large mixing bowl. Mix half of the fruit purée with the crème fraîche and add the borage flowers. Layer into four individual glasses or bowls alternate spoonfuls of fruit purée and the crème fraîche mixture until each glass is full. Decorate each container with three flowers and chill in refrigerator before serving.

Calendula officinalis
POT MARIGOLD

❖

Annual, Ht. 60cm (24in). Single or double daisy-like flower, orange or yellow in colour. Flowering from spring until the first frosts. The flowers have a mild, bitter flavour. Light-green, lance-shaped leaves.

This jolly annual flower livens up any garden or container. It has been used as an edible flower for many years. The Egyptians were the first recorded eaters of it, followed by the Arabs and Indians. The Greeks and Romans also treated marigolds as the poor man's saffron, flavouring and colouring their food with the petals. More recently it has been used to colour butter.

HOW TO GROW
SEED
Sow these easy-to-handle seeds in autumn under protection in a seed or plug tray. Alternatively wait until spring when the soil has begun to warm up. Sow direct into the garden in rows or clusters, thinning to 30-45cm (12-16in) apart. If you live in a very hot climate flowering may become a bit erratic and the plant straggly. Dead-head vigorously to encourage flowering into the autumn.

WHERE TO PLANT
GARDEN
The marigold is a very tolerant plant and will grow in any soil except waterlogged conditions, preferring a sunny position. Plant out in spring when the soil has started to warm and all threat of frost has gone. Beware: this annual does self-seed abundantly.

CONTAINER
Marigolds grow well in pots combining with other plants. They are ideal for window boxes, but not so good in hanging baskets. Position either in semi-shade or full sun. Deadhead flowers to encourage more blooms.

WHEN TO HARVEST
Pick the flowers just as they open during the late spring and summer, both for fresh use and for drying. The petals can be dried (see drying flowers, p146) and kept in a sealed dark container in a cool dry place. Before adding the petals to any recipe pulverise them to release the flavour and colour. Alternatively they can be preserved in butter and oil (see p138).

CULINARY
It is important to pick the petals off this flower and use these as the centre tastes very bitter.

Marigold petals combine well with cheese dishes, and can be used with great effect in salads and omelettes. They make an interesting cup of tea, and, as history indicates, they make a very good food dye. Simply chop the petals up very, very finely, or pulverise using a pestle and mortar, and add this paste to rice dishes, butter – in fact any foods for which you want a lovely golden colour. Also you can make a colourful oil (see floral oils, p142) or simply use the petals as decoration.

My son has always loved cooking: making scones was a Sunday treat and Alistair's Marigold Scones (see opposite) was one of our fun recipes which looks and tastes lovely.

TIP
The sap has the reputation that, when applied to warts, corns and calluses, it will remove them.

OPPOSITE: Serve marigold scones just with butter to capture the flavour of the petals.

ALISTAIR'S MARIGOLD SCONES

Makes about eight scones
450g (1lb) plain flour
1 teaspoon salt
1 teaspoon bicarbonate of soda
45g (1½oz) butter
300ml (½ pint) milk mixed with
2 teaspoons cream of tartar
2 tablespoons fresh marigold petals
Preheat oven to 220°C, 425°F,
gas mark 7

Sift the flour into a bowl with the salt and bicarbonate of soda. Rub in the butter and add the milk and the cream of tartar and the marigold petals. Mix thoroughly until a soft dough is formed. Turn onto a floured board, knead lightly, then roll to about 2cm (¾in) thick. Use a 5cm (2in) plain cutter to cut out the scones and put them on a lightly floured baking sheet. Put in the oven for 12-15 minutes until risen and a golden brown. Cool on a baking tray and eat!

ORECCHIETTE AND MARIGOLDS

Serves 2-4
185g (6½oz) orecchiette pasta
1 tablespoon olive oil
1 clove of garlic, peeled and crushed
2 tablespoons marigold petals

Bring a large pan of water to the boil and add salt if required. Pour the orecchiette slowly into the boiling water and stir. Boil for 10–12 minutes until tender. Drain well. Put the olive oil into the pan, heat gently and add the crushed garlic and the cooked orecchiette, and toss. Then add the marigold petals. Put into a serving dish and serve either hot or cold with salads and cheese.

Chamaemelum nobile
CHAMOMILE

❖

Perennial, Ht. 15cm (6in). Sweet, apple-scented white daisy flowers with a yellow centre. Aromatic, finely divided foliage.

Chamomile has been used for centuries, the most common way being chamomile tea, made from the flowers. It also combines well with fruit dishes and cream or light cheeses.

There is a lot of confusion in identifying the different chamomile species. Firstly, *Chamaemelum nobile* 'Treneague', lawn chamomile, grows close to the ground, does not flower and therefore does not grow from seed. It can be propagated only from cuttings. *Chamaemelum nobile* 'Flore Pleno', double flowered chamomile, is very low growing with a double white flower, the petals of which are edible. *Matricaria recutita*, German chamomile, or may weed, is an annual with scented white flowers and finely scented leaves. The main use of this chamomile is medicinal; the flowers taste, to put it politely, of the 'farmyard'.

TIP

Chamomile planted next to ailing plants can help to revive them.

HOW TO GROW

SEED
Sow these fine seeds on the surface of a prepared seed or plug tray. Cover with perlite. If starting off inside, before the weather has begun to warm, use a bottom heat of 19°C (65°F).

DIVISION
All established perennial chamomile plants of two years or more benefit from being divided in the spring and replanted.

WHERE TO PLANT

GARDEN
Although chamomile prefers a well-drained soil in a sunny situation they will tolerate partial shade. Plant at a distance of 15cm (6in) apart.

CONTAINER
The white daisy flowers look very cheerful in a window box or large container. Use well-draining compost.

WHEN TO HARVEST
Pick the flowers just as the petals slightly droop. Dry fast (see p146), and once dried, remove the leaves and stems and store the flowers in a dark, tight-sealing container.

CULINARY
I know it is presumed that everyone knows how to make a herbal tea, but, just in case, I give a quick recipe on p36. You can use fresh flowers as easily as dried; make sure the petals are just turning back to get the best flavour. Younger flowers have a lighter flavour.

CHAMOMILE FRUIT SALAD

Serves 4
4 peaches
6 Victoria plums
3 figs
3 apples
1 dessertspoon chamomile petals

Wash, core, remove stones, peel and slice all the fruit as necessary. Put into a serving bowl. Make the chamomile tea as in the recipe on p36, adding the honey and the slice of lemon. Cover and let it stand for 20 minutes. Strain the cooled tea and pour it over the fruit salad. Sprinkle over the chamomile petals and serve.

CHAMOMILE TEA

1 heaped teaspoon chamomile flowers,
fresh or dried
1 teaspoon honey (for those with a
sweet tooth)
1 slice of lemon (for those of you who
want a zing)

Put the chamomile flowers into a warm
cup. Pour over boiling water. Cover
and allow to stand (infuse) for three to
five minutes. Strain and add the honey
or lemon if required. Drink either hot
or cold.

Double flowered chamomile also makes a
good cuppa

Chrysanthemum coronarium
CHOPSUEY GREEN, GARLAND CHRYSANTHEMUM

❖

Hardy annual, Ht. 45cm (18in). Flowers all summer, the colour varying from all yellow, to white and yellow. They have a bitter, clean taste. The chrysanthemum-shaped leaves have a spicy flavour.

Chopsuey green or garland chrysanthemum is the least bitter of all the Chrysanthemum family. The petals and the whole young flowers are lovely in stir-fry dishes and cooked with marrows. The petals make a good addition to salads, especially ones using peppers, and can also be floated on top of soups to make ravishingly pretty and refreshing servings. The whole flower makes an ideal garnish. A point of information: *Chrysanthemum* Pot Mum (which is also edible but can be bitter) has had its Latin reclassified to *Dendranthema* ssp.

HOW TO GROW

SEED
Sow the seeds on the surface of a prepared seed or plug tray. Cover with perlite. If starting off inside, before the weather has started to warm up, use a bottom heat of 19°C (65°F).

WHERE TO PLANT

GARDEN
Chopsuey can grow fairly tall so position it in the middle of the border or herb garden. It is happier in a sunny position in a rich, moist, well-drained soil. The root system is shallow so can tolerate stony ground; however you will need to feed regularly to get a good crop. This plant is very tolerant of temperature variation. In temperatures of 21-32°C (70-90°F) it will grow very rapidly, which means one can cut it back and usually get two crops of flowers, if not three

with a bit of feeding with a liquid fertiliser after each cutting back. It can also withstand a frost of -4°C (25°F) and still come back to give a leaf crop, if given a bit of cosseting.

CONTAINER
These chrysanthemums are very good value for money. They look grand in large containers and, by planting four or five plants in a large pot, 30cm (12in) in diameter, they will give a show of flowers from early summer through to the first hard frosts. You should be able to get three crops in the season, if you feed after each cut back.

WHEN TO HARVEST
Pick when the flower first fully opens and place in water. Remove the petals just before using in a salad or in stir-fry dishes, remembering to remove the white heel from the petals because this

is the truly bitter part. If you want to use the whole flower, first make sure it is young, remove as much green as possible, and wash carefully to remove any insects. Pat dry on kitchen towel.

CULINARY
This, in my opinion, is an under-used plant, for the leaves in their own right are great in salads and stir-fry dishes, and the flower is really a bonus. It is the only truly edible chrysanthemum. The petals are good in oils (see p142) and butters (see p138) if you want a slightly bitter/spicy tang. The whole flower is better cooked than raw, so if you want to add it whole to a green salad, quickly and lightly fry some cleaned flowers in vegetable oil or butter, and then toss them into the salad. In the following recipe I use the petals and flowers for the main dish with extra flowers as a garnish.

OPPOSITE: whole stir-fried flowers taste wonderful, left uncooked they can be bitter; so if you want to eat them raw, just add the petals

STIR FRY CHOPSUEY WITH BEAN SPROUTS, ORANGE AND GREEN AND YELLOW PEPPERS

Serves 4

*3 coloured peppers (you can use
all the same but different colours
are prettier and quite often
the supermarkets have mixed packs
on offer)
1 tablespoon vegetable oil
1 large onion, chopped
8 whole chopsuey green flowers (refer
to 'When to Harvest', left, for
preparation instructions)
2 tablespoons chopsuey green petals
150g (5oz) bean sprouts, washed
1 tablespoon soya sauce*

Prepare the peppers by removing the seeds, white pith and green stalk. Slice them. Heat the oil in a heavy frying pan, and sauté the onion gently until translucent. Toss in the sliced peppers and fry quickly for two minutes, stirring all the time. Add the flowers, petals, bean sprouts and soya sauce. Fry for a further minute then serve immediately. Garnish with extra flowers if required. Serve with boiled rice.

TIP

Even if you are not going to use all the flowers it is essential to pick them off as this will promote new growth and more flowers.

Cichorium intybus
CHICORY

❖

Hardy perennial, Ht. 1m (3ft). Clear, stunning blue flowers from mid-summer to mid-autumn. Mid-green hairy leaves.

One sees this beautiful flower growing in lime-rich sites by the sides of the roads and canals of Europe. The flowers have a mild, lettuce-like flavour, making them lovely in any salads where a gentle but not overpowering flavour is wanted. They will lighten the heart of any salad. Look out for *Cichorium intybus album*, white chicory and *Cichorium intybus roseum*, pink chicory; both are good. A combination of pink, white and blue flowers really can look spectacular in a salad.

HOW TO GROW

SEED

Sow the small seeds thinly either in spring or late summer in prepared pots or plug trays. For rapid germination (seven to ten days), sow when freshest, in late summer. Winter the young plants under cover in a cold greenhouse or cold frame. Plant out as soon as all threat of frost has passed at a distance of 45cm (18in) apart.

WHERE TO PLANT

GARDEN

Chicory can be sown direct into a sunny open site with light, preferably alkaline, soil. Thin the seedling to 15-20cm (6-8in) apart in mid- to late summer. If transplanting, do this as early as possible, remembering that chicory grows tall. Position it at the back of a border or against a fence to protect it from the wind, making sure it gets plenty of sun; the flowers open at sunrise and close at sunset.

CONTAINER

Chicory, being tall, is not ideally suited to container growing. However it is possible if you position the container next to a wall and allow the plant to lean against it as it grows.

WHEN TO HARVEST

Chicory flowers are very like dandelion flowers, in-as-much as, when you pick them and bring them

inside, they close, so when using for a salad pick and serve them as quickly as possible.

CULINARY

I have yet to find a way of successfully preserving these delicate flowers. The flavour is too delicate to make an oil or sugar. The whole flower can be eaten, if you make sure all the green bits have been removed beforehand. They look very pretty in a butter or frozen in ice cubes. Use the flowers in green salads and fruit salads, both suit the flavour of the flower.

TIP

Do not forget that the young leaves are equally good in salads, and that the root can be roasted and then ground as a substitute for coffee. In addition young roots can be dug up, boiled and served with a sauce as a vegetable in its own right.

then the chicory leaves, then the Little Gem and top with the lamb's lettuce. Make the salad dressing by mixing the dill and oil together and then whisking in the vinegar. Season to taste. Pour over the salad, scatter the chicory flowers over the top. Toss and serve.

CHICORY FLOWER AND SARDINE-STUFFED LEMONS

This is a great way to make a starter.

Serves 6
6 large lemons
100g (4oz) unsalted butter, softened
6 fresh sardines
1 teaspoon tomato paste
1 teaspoon French mustard
1 pinch grated nutmeg
8 blue chicory flowers

Cut a thin slice off the bottom of each lemon so they stand up on their own. Cut a large slice off the top so you can scoop out the flesh with a sharp-edged spoon. Persevere to remove any tough membranes and pips. Keep the juice and the pulp. Put the butter in a food processor and blend until creamy. Add the sardines, the tomato paste, lemon pulp and juice and mustard and blend until all the ingredients are smooth, then add the nutmeg. Remove the petals from two of the chicory flowers and stir into the mixture. Spoon into the lemons, put a flower on the top and cover with the lemon top. Chill before serving. Arrange on a plate and decorate with any remaining flowers.

GREEN LEAF SALAD WITH BLUE, PINK AND WHITE CHICORY FLOWERS

There are no hard and fast rules to making this salad and the ingredients given here are only suggestions.

Serves 4
1 moss curled endive
1 lamb's lettuce (corn salad)
1 Cos-type lettuce (Little Gem)
1 crisp lettuce (Webb's Wonderful)
5 young chicory leaves
10 different-coloured chicory flowers, with green bits removed

Salad dressing
1 tablespoon dill, chopped
3 tablespoons olive oil
1 tablespoon tarragon vinegar
Freshly ground salt and pepper

Wash, dry and break the lettuce leaves into a salad bowl. Line the bowl with the Webb's, then the curled endive,

Citrus sinensis and Citrus limon
ORANGE and LEMON
❖

Evergreen tree/bush, Ht. up to 8m (25ft). Small, highly aromatic, white, star-shaped flowers either single or in clusters in spring.

The citrus flower is sometimes quite overwhelming in scent and flavour. It is sweet, pungent and citrus all in one. So, as one can imagine, it goes well with lots of different foods from stir-fry to puddings.

HOW TO GROW
SEED
Citrus plants can be grown from seed. However be warned that the resultant seedlings are slow to bear fruit and may not be true. Sow in a prepared small pot using a bark, peat compost mix. As soon as seedlings are established, transfer to pots with a loam-based compost, making sure the compost is pressed down firmly. This will prevent the wood of the plant becoming soft and too sappy and not ripening properly.

CUTTINGS
Cuttings can be taken of semi-ripe shoots from late spring to early summer. Use a bark, peat and grit mix of compost. When rooted and established, pot up into a loam-based compost and press down firmly as above.

WHERE TO PLANT
GARDEN
Both oranges and lemons have been successfully grown outdoors in southern England in a well-sheltered garden against a south-facing wall. The fruit crop is not usually worth writing home about. The soil needs to be warm, rich, moist and well drained. In warm climates the trees need to be planted 5-6m (15-20ft) apart and kept well watered. A tree will reach its full potential in approximately ten years, cropping up to 500 fruits per tree per annum.

CONTAINER
In a northern European climate, it is advisable to grow citrus plants in containers, leaving them out in the summer and bringing them into a glasshouse or conservatory in the autumn. Plant in a large container using a loam-based compost that is well drained. Prune in the spring and early autumn to maintain shape. Do not let the pot dry out and keep well watered in summer.

WHEN TO HARVEST
Pick the flowers as they come into flower and when in full flower. They can be dried or frozen but are best preserved in sugar, oil, syrup or butter (see p138).

CULINARY
These sweet, pungent flowers are lovely in both savoury and sweet dishes. The whole flower is edible but make sure you detach the green bits. If you are sensitive to pollen, remove the centre stamens and just eat the petals.

TIP
If your tree does set fruit it will take up to one year to ripen, so be patient!

GREEN THAI CHICKEN CURRY WITH CITRUS FLOWERS AND RICE

Serves 6

1 roasting chicken, approx.
1.5kg (3lb)
300ml (½ pint) each, thick and thin
coconut milk
(see below)
3 tablespoons green curry paste
(see below)
2 sprigs tender citrus leaves
(lemon or orange)
2 tablespoons fresh green chillies,
finely chopped, seeds removed
1 teaspoon salt
4 tablespoons fresh coriander leaves,
finely chopped
3 tablespoons citrus flowers,
for decoration

To make coconut milk
340g (12oz) desiccated coconut
1.1 litres (2 pints) water

Put two cups of desiccated coconut in a large bowl, heat 600ml (1 pint) water and pour over. Allow to cool to lukewarm, knead firmly for a few minutes and strain through a fine sieve, squeezing out as much liquid as possible. Keep this liquid to one side as thick coconut milk. Then repeat, using the same coconut and adding another 600ml (1 pint) of hot water. This second liquid is thin coconut milk.

To make green curry paste
4 large fresh chillies, seeds removed
(unless you want to blast your head off)
1 teaspoon black peppercorns
1 small onion
1 tablespoon garlic, chopped
2 tablespoons fresh coriander
1 teaspoon coriander seed, ground
1 teaspoon cumin, ground
1 teaspoon turmeric, ground
1 tablespoon oil

Put all the ingredients into a mixer and blend until smooth, adding extra oil if necessary. If you do not have time, you can buy good curry paste.

Divide the chicken into joints. Heat 300ml (½ pint) thick coconut milk slowly until it comes to the boil, lower the heat and continue to cook, stirring all the time until it becomes thick. Add three tablespoons of the green curry paste and cook for a further five minutes, stirring all the time. Add the chicken joints to the curry sauce, turning them until they change colour, and then add 300ml (½ pint) of the thin coconut milk and the citrus leaves. Stir until the mixture boils

43

orange pulp in the saucepan and bring slowly to the boil, stirring from time to time to make sure the sugar does not stick to the bottom. Simmer for approximately eight minutes.

Strain this liquid and check for sweetness. If it is too sour add some more sugar. Allow to cool before pouring into a freezing tray and putting in the freezer. Leave for ten minutes, then using a whisk or fork, mash it up. Keep doing this until the mixture resembles a slush. Then mix the whisked egg white well into the

slush and add a further tablespoon of flowers. Spoon the mixture into the frozen orange skin shells and put back in the freezer.

Take out of the freezer ten minutes or so before serving and decorate with the remaining tablespoon of flowers.

OPPOSITE: Orange Sorbet

TOP LEFT: newly-formed oranges

BELOW: orange flowers

again, then turn the heat low and simmer, uncovered, for about 35 minutes or until the chicken is well cooked and the sauce rich and oily. Stir in the fresh chillies, salt and herbs and simmer for five more minutes.

Serve with plain, boiled rice and garnish with citrus flowers.

ORANGE SORBETS
Serves 4

4 large oranges (preferably unwaxed)
300ml (½ pint) water
75g (3oz) granulated sugar
3 tablespoons orange flowers
1 egg white, whisked

Cut the tops off the oranges and scoop out the pulp into a saucepan. Put the orange skin shells into the freezer to use later as serving bowls.

Add the water, sugar and one tablespoon of orange flowers to the

Coriandrum sativum
CORIANDER
❖

Tender annual, Ht. 60cm (24in). Small white flowers in summer. The first and lower leaves are broad with a strong scent and flavour; the upper leaves are finely cut with a more pungent smell.

You should normally try and inhibit flowering to help the plant produce more leaf, but as it is nearly impossible to stop coriander flowering, it is a real relief to know that the flowers taste marvellous and can be used. The flavour is a combination of the upper and lower leaves, slightly sweeter with a nut undertone. They are great in many dishes, from Thai cooking and salads to soups and dips.

HOW TO GROW
SEED
These seeds are easily handled and should be sown directly into prepared plug trays or pots. Do not use seed trays because coriander hates its roots being disturbed when being transplanted and, if you do, it will bolt very quickly, missing out the leaf stage. Plant the young plants out in the garden when the soil has warmed and all threat of frost has gone, 23cm (9in) apart. If you are just growing coriander for leaf production, then 5cm (2in) apart will be sufficient.

WHERE TO PLANT
GARDEN
As soon as the soil begins to warm, after the threat of frost is over, sow direct into the ground in shallow drills in a light, well-drained soil in a sunny position. When the plant reaches the flowering stage it will be about 60cm (24in) tall and will need support if the site is windy.

CONTAINER
As coriander dislikes being transplanted it is better to sow directly into the container in which you intend to grow it. The main advantage of container growing is that you can control the environment in which coriander grows, protecting it from frost and too much cold rain. Wherever you choose to position the container, ensure that it is in full sun or strong light to stop the plant becoming leggy.

WHEN TO HARVEST
Pick coriander flowers as and when they appear. They can be preserved in oil, butter or vinegar (see p138). All three have merits and are worth doing.

CULINARY
Coriander flowers are more adaptable than the leaves or seed, combining well with so many different dishes. They are lovely whole in a cream cheese dip, added at the end of a stir-fry dish or scattered on the top of cauliflower. There really are endless possibilities, especially if you include the oil, butter and vinegar. Use the oil as the base of a moussaka, combine the leaf, seed and flowers with mushrooms in a tomato sauce and use in pasta dishes. Use the coriander oil and vinegar to make a different French dressing. If you are feeling adventurous scatter the flowers over an orange fruit salad; you will find the flavour of the flower complements the tang of the orange.

TIP
The seed is equally good to use and eat. On ripening they develop a delightful orangey scent and have a warm spicy flavour. I consider that home-grown seeds are markedly superior to those raised commercially because they taste so much fresher and more orangey.

CORIANDER FLOWERS IN A TOMATO JELLY SALAD

Serves 4

6 large tomatoes
1 teaspoon chopped shallot
1 teaspoon fresh thyme, chopped
2 teaspoons fresh coriander leaves,
chopped
Freshly ground black pepper
1 onion, peeled and sliced
1 bay leaf
2 cloves
1 tablespoon tomato paste
4 tablespoons hot water
1 teaspoon salt
1 sachet of gelatine or 2 teaspoons of
agar powder if you are vegetarian
1 tablespoon coriander flowers

Put the tomatoes, shallot, thyme, coriander leaves, pepper, onion, bay leaf and cloves into a pan. Slowly bring to the boil and simmer until the tomatoes are soft. Then stir in the tomato paste, hot water and salt. Simmer for three minutes, stirring from time to time. Strain through a sieve, return the mixture to a pan and slowly bring to boiling point. Add the gelatine and stir until dissolved. Add the coriander flowers, stir and then pour the liquid into a 1.25 litre (2¼ pint) round jelly ring mould. Chill until set.

To serve, turn the mould out onto a serving dish. In the centre of the ring you can put either lots of coriander flowers, a potato salad, a sliced green salad or chopped cold meats, whatever you like.

CORIANDER FLOWERS AND PRAWNS

Serves 4-6

450g (1lb) peeled, cooked prawns
6 tablespoons lemon juice
6 spring onions, sliced in rounds
2 teaspoons fresh ginger, peeled
and grated
2 tablespoons coriander flowers
1 tablespoon mint, finely chopped
1 tablespoon coriander leaves,
finely chopped

Put the prawns into a bowl and pour over the lemon juice. If you are using frozen prawns make sure they are thoroughly defrosted first. Stir in the spring onion, ginger, coriander leaves, mint, and a tablespoon of the coriander flowers. Cover and put in the refrigerator for a couple of hours before serving. When ready to serve, place the prawns and their sauce in a serving bowl or on individual serving plates and garnish with the remaining coriander flowers.

Cucurbita pepo var.
COURGETTE OR MARROW

❖

Annual, Ht. 30-45cm (12-18in). Yellow to cream-coloured, trumpet-shaped flowers in summer, with a soft vegetative flavour. Green maple-shaped leaves.

There are many varieties of marrow, which include those that grow in a bush, and those that trail. There are courgettes, which are only marrows picked very young, and there are squashes of all different shapes and colours. All have one thing in common: they all produce flowers which are yellow in colour, but of varying size. There are male flowers and female flowers. It is easy to tell the difference as male flowers are on long slender stems and female flowers are on very short stems and you will see the baby marrow appearing behind the flower. If you use the female flower before it has been pollinated the baby marrow will wither and turn brown.

HOW TO GROW
SEED
Sow the seeds in early spring into prepared small pots or large plug trays, not seed trays because marrows hate having their roots disturbed when being transplanted. Ideally put two seeds per 9cm (4in) pot. If the temperature is still cold, a bottom heat of 18°C (65°F) will help germination.

WHERE TO PLANT
GARDEN
Seeds can be sown direct into the ground in a well-prepared, sunny site with a rich soil. It is best to dig holes 30cm (12in) square and fill them with a mixture of well-rotted manure or compost. Marrow roots do not go very deep, so no need for a deep hole. Position the holes at a distance 90cm (3ft) apart for bush marrows, 120cm (4ft) apart for trailers and 50cm (20in) apart for courgettes. Sow as soon as the soil has begun to warm and all threat of frost has gone.

CONTAINER
As smaller growers and smaller plants, courgettes are fairly easy to grow in pots provided the pot is large enough to accommodate the root system e.g. 20cm (8in). Window boxes also give space for the courgettes to grow.

WHEN TO HARVEST
Harvest the male flowers when they are just opening as required in summer. However, harvest the female flowers only if you have enough marrows or courgettes.

CULINARY
Wash the flowers carefully, checking there are no earwigs inside. The shape of these yellow trumpet flowers lends itself to being filled with cheese, nuts, bulgar wheat and herbs in any combination. Equally the flowers make a good vegetable dish on their own. A good, quick recipe, if you have a lot of flowers, is to fry an onion and some garlic in oil. Once they are softened, add some courgette flowers and stir-fry until translucent. Toss in some chopped basil and serve.

TIP
Marrows can suffer from a number of pests and diseases, the most common being slugs. Either put beer traps down or go out of an evening with a torch and teach them to fly.

STUFFED COURGETTE FLOWERS

Serves 4-6
10 large courgette flowers
Oil for frying

Batter
100g (4oz) plain flour
Salt
2 tablespoons thyme oil
150ml (¼ pint) warm water
1 egg white

Stuffing
1 tablespoon thyme oil (or olive oil)
1 small onion, peeled and finely chopped
1 clove of garlic, crushed
100g (4oz) cooked brown rice
1 tablespoon pine nuts
1 tablespoon lemon thyme, chopped
Salt & freshly ground black pepper
1 dessertspoon chives, chopped
140ml (5fl oz) low-fat cream cheese

Wash and dry the flowers carefully. To make the batter, sift the flour into a large bowl, add a pinch of salt, stir in the oil and the lukewarm water. The mixture should be like double cream (if necessary add a little extra water). Let this mixture stand for one or two hours before use. When you need it, whip the egg white not too dry and fold it into the batter mixture.

To make the stuffing, heat the thyme oil in a large frying pan, gently fry the onion, add the garlic and continue cooking for one minute. Then add the rice, pine nuts, and thyme and mix together over the heat for two minutes. Remove from the heat, season with freshly ground salt and pepper, add the chopped chives and stir in the cream cheese.

Fill the flowers gently by separating the petals and spooning a little filling into each. Cover the filling with the petals. Dip each filled flower into the batter, scraping the excess off on the edge of the bowl. Heat a large pan with oil to 185°C (360°F) and put in the stuffed flowers, a few at a time. Cook for four minutes, turning once. Drain on kitchen towel and serve immediately.

BELOW: courgette goldrush – the fruit tastes as good as its green counterpart.

Dianthus & ssp.
PINKS
❖

Perennial, Ht.15-60cm (6-24in). Very fragrant white, pink, dark crimson or cerise flower, or a combination of all four. Frilly edges, double and single flowered, with lance-shaped green leaves.

There is nothing more nostalgic than the scent of pinks wafting through a summer's evening. Truly they taste as good as they smell – a sweet clove flavour – lovely in puddings, from fruit pies to fruit salads, or in cakes, jams and jellies. Any dish that needs a fragrant boost can benefit. There are many varieties of *Dianthus*. They are all edible after removing the white heel from the petal. Look out for *Dianthus* 'Mrs Sinkins', or *Dianthus* 'Gran's Favourite' or *Dianthus* 'Prudence', to name a few.

HOW TO GROW
SEED
Pinks can be grown from seed, but they will be very variable in height, colour and habit. This can be fun if you are not being a purist. Sow the small seed in autumn in a prepared seed or plug tray. Winter under cover. When germination starts, it is crucial not to over-water the young plants.

DIVISION
After flowering in the early autumn, established plants can be dug up and divided.

CUTTINGS
Softwood cuttings can be taken in the spring. Alternatively, heel cuttings are best taken in the early autumn.

WHERE TO PLANT
GARDEN
Pinks prefer a well-drained soil, low in plant nutrient, and a sunny sheltered site.

CONTAINER
Pinks look most attractive in old terracotta pots. Use a free-draining compost and in winter keep the compost on the dry side.

WHEN TO HARVEST
Pick the flowers as they open. Preserve by adding the petals to sugar, syrups, jams, oils, vinegars or by crystallising (see p138).

CULINARY
This versatile flower is simple to use. For all dishes, remove the petals from the flower, then remove the white heel at the base of the petal as this has a very bitter taste.

TIP
The main pest is the red spider mite. As soon as you see it, treat with a horticultural soap, following the manufacturer's instructions.

LEFT: this wonderful vase sets off the Cheddar pinks brilliantly

PINK JAM

Makes approx. 700g

200g (7oz) granulated sugar
300ml (½ pint) water
50g (2oz) Dianthus petals, prepared

Put the sugar and water into a saucepan and bring slowly to the boil, stirring until the sugar has dissolved, and simmer until it thickens. Add the chopped petals, stirring all the time, and slowly simmer until the mixture is very thick. Pour into sterilised warmed jars, allow to cool, cover. Once opened, keep refrigerated and use within three to four weeks.

PINKS WITH CREME FRAICHE AND FRUIT SALAD

Serves 4

1 honeydew melon
225g (8oz) lychees
2 kiwi fruit, peeled and sliced
24 gooseberries, previously cooked
225g (8oz) green seedless grapes
1 tablespoon Dianthus petals, white heels removed
150ml (¼ pint) white grape juice.
4 Dianthus flowers for decoration

For Crème Fraîche

200ml (6¾ fl oz) crème fraîche
2 tablespoons Dianthus petals, with the white heels removed

To make the salad, scoop the melon flesh out in balls or use a dessertspoon. Peel, stone and halve the lychees. Mix all the fruit together in a bowl, add the grape juice and the petals. Stir and chill in the refrigerator for a couple of hours before serving. Just before serving, mix the petals with the crème fraîche in a bowl and then chill in the refrigerator. Before serving, decorate the crème fraîche and the salad with whole flowers.

BELOW: Pinks with crème fraîche and fruit salad

Eruca vesicaria ssp. *sativa*
SALAD ROCKET

❖

Annual, Ht. 60-90cm (2-3ft). In summer the four-petalled flower starts yellow, then, as it ages, becomes whiter with purple veins. The leaves are oval, lance-shaped and mid-green.

This plant is known by many different common names, for example arugula, rocquette, rugola and rucola. With a plant which has a tendency to bolt into flower, it is a definite bonus if the flower tastes excellent. Salad rocket flowers certainly do, and the flavour is a mixture of crunchy nut, pepper and beef. They add an exotic touch to savoury and stir-fry dishes, as well as to sweet ones in which they should be used with discretion. For instance, after some interesting trial and error, I have found that they combine well with rhubarb fool.

HOW TO GROW
SEED
This plant is better grown direct in the garden.

WHERE TO PLANT
GARDEN
As this plant has two distinct crops, leaf and flower, think which you want at the time of sowing the seed. The soil should be moist and lightly shaded for leaf production and in full sun for flower production. Sow direct into the garden, in prepared rows, as soon as all threat of frost has gone and the soil has started to warm. In temperate countries salad rocket can be sown in autumn for an extra crop of winter leaves; in cooler climates, sow in early spring for a summer harvest. If you do not have the space to grow rows of salad rocket, sow the seed in little clumps, in the flower border. Thin the seedlings to 20cm (8in) for both leaf and flower production. The leaf should be ready to pick within six to eight weeks of sowing and the flower within 12 to 14 weeks. The later in the season the sowing, i.e. the warmer it is, the more likely the plant will run quickly to flower.

CONTAINER
Salad rocket does not grow very happily in containers as a leaf crop. For flowers, it is a different matter; sow directly into the pot and position in a sheltered place, otherwise the tall stems will need staking to avoid being blown over. The warmth encourages flowering. Keep well watered. If you keep picking the flowers new ones will form, so there will be a harvest all summer long.

WHEN TO HARVEST
For the best flavour pick the flowers in the early yellow stage. Use them fresh; they do not dry, but can be preserved in oil, vinegars and butter (see p138).

CULINARY
The whole flower is edible although any excessive green should be removed. The swelling behind the flower (where the seeds are formed) adds the crunch when eating the flower. So use just petals, whole flowers, or whole flowers plus crunch depending on the recipe. Try adding them to rice salads, or scatter them over cooked French beans before serving. A very good combination is to add whole flowers to taramasalata, and serve with hot brown toast.

TIP
Watch out for flea beetle; if you notice little holes appearing in the leaves then you have this pest. Use soot around the plants as soon as you see an attack.

YOGHURT TOPPING FOR JACKET POTATOES

Serves 4
4 jacket potatoes
150ml (½ pint) plain yoghurt
18 salad rocket leaves, finely chopped
10 salad rocket flowers, plus crunch
1 tablespoon salad rocket flowers
(no crunch)

Cook the jacket potatoes in the oven until ready. Put the yoghurt in a bowl, add the rocket leaves and the flowers with crunch and mix together thoroughly. When the potatoes are cooked, remove from oven, slice open with a cross in the top. Put a tablespoon of the yoghurt mixture on each potato and sprinkle with the remaining flowers. Put the remaining mixture in a small bowl and, if any flowers are left, sprinkle on the top. Serve immediately.

RED, GREEN AND YELLOW SALAD

Serves 2-4
1 green pepper
1 red onion
10 salad rocket flowers with crunch
1 tablespoon salad rocket
flower petals
30-40 salad rocket leaves

Salad dressing
3 tablespoons olive oil
(or sunflower)
1 tablespoon tarragon vinegar
1 tablespoon French Dijon mustard
Salt and pepper to taste

Slice the pepper finely and cut the onion into rings. Gently wash the salad rocket flowers, extra petals and leaves, and pat dry on kitchen towel. Incorporate all these ingredients in a salad bowl.

Make the salad dressing by whisking the oil, vinegar and mustard together. Season to taste. Pour over the salad, toss and serve.

55

Filipendula ulmaria
MEADOWSWEET
❖

Perennial, Ht. 60-120cm (2-4ft). Clusters of creamy-white, sweetly-scented flowers in mid-summer. Green leaf made up of five pairs of big leaflets.

The flowers of this plant have been used since Anglo-Saxon times. In Chaucer's *The Knight's Tale* 'Meadwort' was one of the ingredients in a drink called 'Save'. Apart from making a great wine the flowers can be added to stewed fruit, jams and vinegars. Anyone who has read my *Complete Herb Book* will recall that meadowsweet vinegar was the first floral vinegar I tried. It was given to me by my charming local vet, and it really does make a good base for vinaigrette salad dressing. The flowers of *Filipendula ulmaria* 'Aurea', golden meadowsweet, and *Filipendula ulmaria* 'Variegata', variegated meadowsweet, are just as edible as common meadowsweet.

MEADOWSWEET WINE

Makes four to five bottles
600ml (1 pint) meadowsweet flowers
(heads only)
225g (8oz) raisins, chopped
1.6kg (3½lb) white sugar
4½ litres (1 gallon) boiling water
Juice of 3 lemons
150ml (¼ pint) strong tea
20g (¾oz) baker's yeast or 1 teaspoon
granulated yeast
1 teaspoon wine-making nutrient
(obtainable from a chemist)

HOW TO GROW
SEED
Sow in prepared seed or plug trays in the autumn. Cover lightly with compost and winter outside under glass. Check occasionally to make sure the compost has not become too dry because this will inhibit germination. When the seedlings are large enough, plant out 30cm (12in) apart.

DIVISION
Established plants can be divided in the autumn and replanted into a prepared site.

WHERE TO PLANT
GARDEN
Plant in semi-shade in a moisture-retentive soil. If your soil dries out in summer add a lot of well-rotted manure and/or leaf mould to the soil before planting.

CONTAINER
The decorative forms of meadowsweet grow smaller than the wild form and both the golden and variegated forms look most attractive in containers. However, position the container in the semi-shade and make sure it does not dry out.

WHEN TO HARVEST
Pick the flowers as soon as they open. Preserve them in vinegar, oils (see opposite) or sugars or make a meadowsweet jelly (see p138).

CULINARY
The rich, sweetly-scented flowers can be eaten in salads but I feel the full flavour does not come across and they are better used in oils, vinegars and jellies. Alternatively, if you enjoy making home brews, I recommend the following recipe.

Place the flowers, raisins and sugar in a plastic bucket with fitting lid. Pour in the water and stir well. When cool add the lemon juice, tea, yeast and nutrient. Ferment for four to five days at 18-20°C (65-70°F), stirring twice daily and keeping it tightly covered. Then strain into a fermentation vessel and fit an air lock. When fermentation finishes and the wine has cleared, rack off into clean bottles and keep for three months before using.

MEADOWSWEET FRITTERS

I am not a great fan of meadowsweet fritters but this recipe is very jolly.

Makes about 16 fritters
(depending on the size of the
flower heads)
*2 heads of meadowsweet flowers
per person
125g (4oz) plain flour
Pinch of salt
1 tablespoon oil
150ml (¼ pint) beer or water
2 small eggs, separated
Oil for frying
Caster sugar for dredging
Chopped rose petals (with their white
heels removed) for garnish*

Prepare the meadowsweet flowers by washing gently under the tap, and gently patting dry on some kitchen towel. Set aside on more clean towel.

Mix the flour and salt with the oil and beer or water, whisking well until smooth, then stir in the egg yolks. Cover and leave in a warm place for a few hours to allow the flour to ferment slightly. Just before using, whisk the egg whites until stiff and fold into the batter. Heat the oil to 220°C (425°F). Shake the flower heads, dip them into the batter and fry until golden brown. Sprinkle with caster sugar and chopped rose petals. The combination of meadowsweet and rose is delicious and the petals finish off this dish delightfully.

ABOVE: meadowsweet preserved in oils

TIP
The flowers make a tea which is beneficial if you are suffering from flu.

Foeniculum vulgare
FENNEL

❖

Perennial, Ht.1.5-2.1m (4-7ft). Lots of small, slightly-scented, yellow flowers in large umbels in late summer. Soft green, aniseed-scented feathery foliage.

These sweet anise-flavoured flowers are great added to fish or pork dishes. They, like the leaves, help to break down the cholesterol in food. The whole plant is edible. It is a plant which has been used in cooking since Roman times and was one of the sacred herbs of the Anglo-Saxons. The flowers of *Foeniculum vulgare* 'Purpureum', bronze fennel, can be used in exactly the same way as those of *Foeniculum vulgare*, green fennel.

HOW TO GROW

SEED

Sow the seed in early spring in prepared pots or plug trays and cover with perlite. A bottom heat of 15°C (60°F) helps speed up germination. Plant out in the garden once all threat of frost has gone.

DIVISION

Division of established stock is only really successful if you have a light, sandy soil. Dig the plant up in autumn, divide and replant in a well-prepared site.

WHERE TO PLANT

GARDEN

Fennel likes a sunny position in a fertile, well-drained light soil. Even though fennel is a perennial, it is advisable to replace the plant every three years. If sowing direct in the garden, sow after the last frosts.

OPPOSITE: fennel with sunflowers

CONTAINER

Foeniculum vulgare 'Purpureum', bronze fennel, looks very attractive in containers. It may need staking when it starts to flower. In summer, shelter from the midday sun, water and feed regularly.

WHEN TO HARVEST

Pick the flower heads when they are fully opened. They can be preserved in oil, vinegar or butter (see p138).

CULINARY

The whole small flower is edible. Remove each one from the umbel stems, leaving just the flower. The sweet aniseed flavour combines well with soups, especially cucumber or potato, with fish dishes where the flavour of the flower combines well with mackerel and many vegetable dishes including potato, tomato and cucumber salad. An oil made from the flowers is very good for frying fish or basting pork chops on a barbeque.

CUCUMBER SALAD
Serves 4
1 large cucumber
2 tablespoons fennel flowers, prepared
1 tablespoon fennel leaves, chopped
1 teaspoon salt

Peel the cucumber, slice very finely and place in a shallow dish. Sprinkle over some salt, cover with a plate and weight it to press down on the cucumber; put aside for one hour. Drain off any excess liquid. Lay the slices out in a serving dish, sprinkle the cucumber with fennel flowers and fennel leaves and serve. This goes very well with poached salmon.

TIP

Do not plant near coriander because the flavour of both plants will be impaired. Fennel tea made from the seeds is used to aid digestion and prevent both heartburn and constipation.

RED CABBAGE AND FENNEL FLOWERS

Serves 4

1 medium red cabbage
2 eating apples, peeled, cored and
roughly chopped
1 tablespoon caster sugar
Butter
2-3 tablespoons fennel flower vinegar
Salt, freshly ground pepper and
freshly grated nutmeg
2 tablespoons fennel flowers, prepared
Preheat oven to 165°C, 325°F,
gas mark 3

Remove the tough, outside leaves of the cabbage, cut into quarters, remove the stalk and slice the leaves into thin shreds. Arrange layers of sliced cabbage with the chopped apple into a well-buttered casserole. Sprinkle each layer with sugar, vinegar, salt, pepper, nutmeg and fennel flowers. Cover and cook for three to three and a half hours. Remove the lid and stir well before serving, scattering the remaining fennel flowers over the top. Serve with pork chops or mackerel and jacket potatoes.

Fuchsia ssp.
FUCHSIA

❖

Deciduous or evergreen shrubs and trees, Ht. up to 2m (7ft). Tubular flowers which are almost always pendulous and often bicolour, from early summer to early autumn. Mid-green oval leaves.

If you have ever seen a display of fuchsias at one of the international flower shows you will appreciate how stunning these vividly coloured blooms are. The range includes single and double flowers, bicolours and even tricolours, pinks and purples all mixed up. I had known for some time that the small black fruits which follow these flowers are used to make jam and jelly but I had no idea until I started this book that the flowers were edible as well. Although the flavour is a bit dull, the few I have tried taste slightly vegetative with an after-zing. They look wonderful crystallised.

HOW TO GROW

SEED
Fuchsias can be raised from seed, but named varieties must be propagated by cuttings. Sow the seed in early autumn or spring into prepared seed or plug trays. When rooted, pot into 8cm (3½in) pots. Protect young plants for the first winter in a cold greenhouse or frame.

CUTTINGS
Softwood cuttings should be taken from young, non-flowering, growing shoots in spring or early autumn and placed into prepared small pots or plug trays. Do not mix the species in the tray or pot. Once established, pot up and keep in pots for the first year.

WHERE TO PLANT
GARDEN
Plant in a sheltered, partially shaded corner of the garden in a moist, fertile well-drained soil. Prolonged low temperatures can cause loss of top growth. If this happens cut back to ground level in the spring.

CONTAINER
Fuchsias look lovely in containers, hanging baskets and window boxes. They need plenty of feeding with a high-nitrogen liquid feed when in flower. Upright species may be trained as compact bushes or standards. Control growth by nipping out the growing tips in summer. Trailing plants are best grown in hanging baskets or, if you are feeling ambitious, they can be trained on trellises. Cut back hard in the autumn and re-pot each spring.

WHEN TO HARVEST
Pick the flowers when they are newly opened. Preserve by crystallising (see p142).

CULINARY
To eat this flower you must not only remove all green and brown bits but also gently remove the stamen and pistils. Either eat the flowers fresh in green salads or fruit salads or crystallise them. This will certainly be a dinner party stopper – who will be brave enough to eat the flower first?

TIP
Keep dead-heading the fuchsia throughout the season and it will keep flowering.

FUCHSIA SALAD

Serves 4

*½ cucumber, peeled in stripes and
chopped*
1 green pepper, deseeded and chopped
*4 tablespoons spearmint or apple
mint, chopped*
1 Cos lettuce, sliced
*50g (2oz) green or gold purslane,
leaves only*
*12 fuchsia flowers, with the stamen,
pistils, and green parts removed*

Salad dressing

3 tablespoons olive oil
*1 tablespoon thyme flower vinegar
or white wine vinegar*
1 clove of garlic, crushed
Salt and pepper to taste

Mix all the salad ingredients in a bowl,
leaving a few flowers to one side. Make
the salad dressing with the oil, vinegar,
garlic and seasoning. Toss the salad
and then arrange the remaining
flowers. Serve immediately.

STRAWBERRY JELLY RING WITH FUCHSIA FLOWERS

Serves 6

675g (1½lb) fresh strawberries
125g (5oz) caster sugar
400ml (14fl oz) water
3 tablespoons gelatine or agar powder
*6 fuchsia flowers, with the stamen,
pistils, and green parts removed*
*12-14 whole strawberries for
decoration*

Put the fruit, sugar and water into a
saucepan and bring to the boil; simmer
for three minutes, stirring. Push the
fruit and liquid through a fine-mesh
sieve to remove all the pips. Return to
the saucepan, heat to just below
boiling and sprinkle the gelatine or
agar powder over the surface. Whisk
until dissolved completely. Stir in the
fuchsia flowers and pour into a 1.25
litre (2¼ pint) metal jelly ring mould.
Allow to cool and then chill for several
hours until firmly set. Turn out onto a
plate. Fill the centre with strawberries.

Helianthus annus
SUNFLOWER

❖

Annual, Ht 30cm-4m (1-12ft). Large, yellow flowers, which can grow to 35cm (14in) in diameter with brown or purple centres. Green, ovate or heart-shaped, coarsely-toothed leaves.

The fields of sunflowers that one can see throughout Europe in mid-summer, all turning their heads to follow the sun, are a truly magnificent sight. The flower buds can be eaten whole; they have a vegetable flavour reminiscent of *Helianthus tuberosus*, Jerusalem artichoke, which is a relation of course. Once the flower opens, only the petals can be eaten, and they have a bittersweet flavour, rather like a souped-up endive. Both the buds and flower petals are delightful in salads, stir-fry and pasta dishes. The perennial varieties also have edible flowers, for example *Helianthus decapetalus*, which has sulphur yellow flowers, and *Helianthus* x *laetiflorus* which has bright yellow flowers. There are many sizes of sunflower available so it is possible to grow them to suit the size of your garden. The section on 'Containers' gives the smaller varieties.

HOW TO GROW
SEED
Sow the seeds either singly in small pots in spring or direct into the garden, after the frosts have finished, 30cm (12in) apart.

DIVISION
Divide the perennial species in either spring or summer.

WHERE TO PLANT
GARDEN
Sunflowers are hardy and easily grown in most soils. However if you want a spectacular 3m (10ft) giant, plant in a well-cultivated and well-fed soil in a sunny position; no sunflowers thrive in shade. The perennial species are gross feeders so it is advisable to lift them every second or third year and replant them in a new site with lots of well-rotted compost.

CONTAINER
It is possible to grow the smaller varieties of sunflowers in containers; these include 'Pacino', a bright yellow variety which grows to 30cm (12in), 'Big Smile' which has yellow petals with a black centre, 30cm (12in), and 'Teddy Bear' which is double flowered and grows to 40cm (15in). Position in full sun and protect from high winds.

WHEN TO HARVEST
Pick the flowers in bud to use whole, or in full flower for the petals, or collect the complete head in early autumn for the seeds.

CULINARY
The buds, petals and seeds are all edible. The golden petals make a lovely contrast when added to a green salad.

TIP
Slugs and rabbits are both equally fond of young sunflower plants, so be warned.

RIGHT: sunflowers are so pretty in borders

SUNFLOWER SEED, PETALS AND PASTA SALAD

Serves 6

350g (12oz) rigatoni
1 tablespoon olive oil
1 clove of garlic, crushed
2 tablespoons sunflower petals
1 tablespoon hazelnuts, chopped
1 tablespoon sunflower seeds
1 dessertspoon chives, chopped
1 tablespoon mayonnaise
Sunflower petals for garnish

Bring a large pan of water to boiling point, add the rigatoni and cook for eight to ten minutes until *al dente*. When cooked, drain. Heat the oil in a large pan, add the garlic and toss in the rigatoni, stir well, remove from the heat and pour into a serving bowl. When cool, cover and chill in the refrigerator. Before serving, mix the sunflower petals, hazelnuts, sunflower seeds and chives into the pasta and then stir in the mayonnaise. Decorate with a few fresh petals and serve.

SUNFLOWER BUDS

This recipe can also be served cold. Omit the melted butter, and serve the buds in a vinaigrette.

Serves 4

8 sunflower buds
30g (1oz) butter, melted
Sunflower petals for garnish

Bring a large pan of water to the boil. Put in the sunflower buds and blanch for two minutes, this will kill any bugs and remove any residual bitterness. Strain them in a colander. Refill the pan with water and bring to the boil. Add the sunflower buds and simmer for a further three minutes until tender, drain, and toss in melted butter. Serve garnished with sunflower petals.

Hemerocallis
DAY LILY

❖

Perennial, Ht.30-90 cm (12-36in). The flowers range in size and colour from pale yellow through to deep red, depending on species. The flowering time also depends on species and is from spring until autumn. All are hardy.

Day lily is a native of Eastern Asia. The name is derived from the fact that each flower lasts for one day only. You will find day lilies in many Chinese recipes from soups to spicy dishes and records show that the flowers have been eaten by the Chinese since early times. The petals, called golden needles, and the buds of the flower are eaten, and both are crisp and crunchy with a fresh taste.

HOW TO GROW

SEED

Many of the species are self-sterile. Either they do not set seed or, if they do, the seedlings will often vary from the parent. So who knows? You could create your own species. Sow the seeds in autumn in a prepared seed or plug tray. In spring, pot up the seedlings and plant out when the soil is warm and free from frost.

DIVISION

Propagate by division in autumn or spring. Divide established plants every three to four years.

WHERE TO PLANT

GARDEN

Plant in full sun and a moist fertile soil. Good for borders and planting in grass (where moist). Some species can take up to two years before they are happily established and start flowering. Feed established plants in the spring with well-rotted manure.

CONTAINER

It is quite possible to grow day lilies in containers; however the container needs to be at least 30cm (12in) in size to ensure it is able to accommodate the plant, bearing in mind the height of the flowers and the large root ball. The mixture of the compost is also important and I recommend using a soil-based mix, as it retains moisture. Plant in the pot, keeping the crown of the plant, where the roots and leaves join, just below the surface of the compost. Too low and the plant will rot, too high and the plant will wilt.

WHEN TO HARVEST

Day lilies open in hot water. So you can pick them in bud, put them in the refrigerator, and then next day plunge them into hot water and watch them open. They can also be frozen in flower or in bud (see p144).

CULINARY

Day lilies are great in salads, hot and

cold soups, cooked and served as a vegetable, chopped up and used in stir-fry dishes. There are many different ways to serve this versatile flower. I found this recipe in a Chinese cookbook and have adapted it to fit my kitchen.

TIP

Slug and snail control is essential in early spring when the young foliage first appears.

BRAISED CHICKEN WITH DAY LILY BUDS AND GINGER

Serves 4-6

*1kg (2lb) oven-ready chicken
(remove meat from bones)
15 fresh or frozen day lily buds
2 tablespoons oil (olive, groundnut
or peanut)
1 piece (4cm/1½in) fresh ginger
1 clove of garlic, crushed*

100ml (3fl oz) dry sherry or
white wine
1 tablespoon honey
50ml (2fl oz) light soy sauce

Cut the chicken into thin, bite-size
pieces. Cut the stem end off the lily
buds and then cut 12 of the buds
into two to three pieces each. Peel
the ginger and grate it on a coarse
grater (mind your fingers). Heat
the oil in a deep frying pan or thick-
based saucepan, and gently fry the
ginger and garlic over a low heat
until they are just starting to brown.
Add the chicken pieces and slowly
increase the heat to medium, stir
the chicken until it changes colour,
add the lily buds, sherry or wine,
honey and soy sauce. Cover the pan
and simmer over a low heat for
25 minutes. You may need to add
a little hot water towards the end
of cooking if the sauce becomes too
dry. Serve with rice and a green
salad. Decorate with the remaining
lily buds.

POTATO SOUP AND DAY LILY FLOWERS

Serves 4
2 leeks
4 day lily buds
40g (1½oz) butter
450g (1lb) potatoes
850ml (1½ pints) chicken stock
Freshly ground salt and pepper
½ teaspoon nutmeg, grated
150ml (¼ pint) single cream

Chop the leeks into rounds and wash
thoroughly. Then put them into a food
processor and chop for a few seconds.
Chop the lily buds into thin slices and
save 12 slices for decoration. Melt the
butter in a large pan, add the leeks
and cook over a low heat until soft.
Peel and roughly chop the potatoes.
Place them in the food processor and
chop finely. Add to the leeks and cook
over a low heat for a few minutes.
Pour over the stock and bring to the

boil, stirring all the time. Simmer
gently for 18 minutes and then add the
sliced lily buds and cook for a further
one minute. Drain off the stock and
reserve. Return the vegetables to the
food processor and purée until
smooth. Add to the stock in a pan, add
the cream and nutmeg, check the
seasoning and heat without boiling.
Serve with three rings of day lily buds
floating on the top of each serving with
a smidgen of cream.

Hesperis matronalis
SWEET ROCKET
❖

Hardy biennial, Ht. 60-90cm (2-3ft). Sweetly scented, mauve, white, pink or purple flowers in the summer of the second year. Green lance-shaped leaves.

These heavenly evening sweet-smelling flowers have a warm scented taste with a hint of violet. They are equally happy in green salads or decorating puddings.

HOW TO GROW

SEED

Sow the seed in autumn in prepared seed or plug trays. Winter the young plants in a cold greenhouse. By sowing early you can sometimes have plants flowering in the first season.

WHERE TO PLANT

GARDEN

Plant in full sun or light shade in a well-drained fertile soil in the middle or towards the back of the border. In late spring, once the soil has begun to warm, you can sow direct into a prepared site in the garden Thin after germination to 30cm (12in) and when well established to the final planting distance of 45cm (18in).

CONTAINER

Sweet rocket is a tall plant, so take this into consideration when potting into containers. Position the container so that you will get the most from the night-scented flowers. When they are fully grown, protect from winds.

WHEN TO HARVEST

Pick the flowers when they open. It is a good idea to pick the complete flowering head. Preserve in butter, sugar, syrup or vinegar (see p138). The whole flower is edible, including the stamen, but minus the stem and any other green bits, so it makes an ideal candidate for crystallising (see p142).

TIP

The young leaves make a very good substitute for salad rocket, but they have a stronger flavour so use sparingly.

CHERRY AND SWEET ROCKET SALAD

Serves 4

450g (1lb) fresh red cherries, stoned
2 lettuce hearts
6 young sweet rocket leaves, chopped
4 tablespoons white sweet rocket flowers (all green bits removed)

Salad dressing

1 egg
60g (2oz) caster sugar
3 tablespoons white wine, sweet rocket flower or tarragon vinegar
Freshly ground salt and pepper
150ml (¼ pint) double cream, lightly whipped

First make the salad dressing: break the egg into a bowl and whisk lightly. Add in the sugar and mix thoroughly. Continue whisking the mixture in the bowl adding the vinegar a small drop at a time and whisking thoroughly each time. Alternatively, if using a food processor, add the vinegar very slowly through the tube, so that the sauce does not curdle. Put this mixture into a small heatproof bowl over a pan of boiling water turned down to simmering point and stir until the mixture begins to thicken. Take off the heat and keep stirring until it has the consistency of thick cream. Remove the basin from the pan and leave to cool, adding the seasoning as required. At this point this mixture can be stored in a screw-top jar for two to three weeks. Add the cream to the salad dressing then gently fold in the cherries. Split the lettuces and arrange on a serving plate. Sprinkle the chopped sweet rocket leaves over the lettuce, spoon on the cherries in the cream dressing and decorate with the sweet rocket flowers.

REDCURRANTS, BLACKCURRANTS AND RASPBERRY YOGHURT ICE CREAM WITH PINK AND MAUVE SWEET ROCKET FLOWERS

Serves 4-6

350g (12oz) mixed redcurrants, blackcurrants and raspberries
90ml (3fl oz) water
50-100g (2-4oz) caster sugar
2 eggs
150 ml (¼ pint) plain yoghurt
10 sweet rocket flowers (with all green bits removed) for ice cream
3 pink and 3 mauve sweet rocket flowers (with all green bits removed) for decoration

Cook the fruit all together, with the water and enough sugar to sweeten, until tender. Gently rub through a sieve to make a purée. Separate the eggs, put the yolks in a bowl and whip until they are smooth and light. Return the purée to a pan and heat to boiling point. Pour very slowly onto the egg yolks, stirring all the time. Keep stirring until all the ingredients are well mixed and light. Add the yoghurt and mix well. Turn into a freezing tray and place in the

ice-making compartment of a refrigerator or in a deep freeze until the mixture is just firm to touch (about one hour). Remove from the freezer and mix until smooth and creamy. Beat the egg whites until stiff and fold in along with the 10 rocket flowers. Return to the freezing trays and freeze until solid.

Take out of the freezer 10 minutes before serving. Scoop into individual bowls and decorate with the remaining rocket flowers.

Hyssopus officinalis
HYSSOP
❖

Perennial, semi-evergreen, Ht. 30-80cm (12-32 in). Blue, scented flowers from summer to early autumn. Small, narrow, aromatic, lance-shaped leaves.

This underrated, under-used culinary herb has small flowers that look lovely gracing many dishes. The pink and white flowering hyssops are just as edible as the blue so all three can be combined in a medley of colours. But beware – the small flowers pack a powerful punch. They have a hot, spicy and thyme-like flavour, so only a small amount is needed in each dish.

HOW TO GROW
SEED
Sow the seed in early spring in prepared seed or plug trays. A bottom heat of 15-21°C (60-70°F) would assist germination. When the seedlings are large enough, either pot up or plant in the garden after all threat of frost has gone.

CUTTINGS
Take softwood cuttings in late spring and early summer from the non-flowering stems.

WHERE TO PLANT
GARDEN
Hyssop is a Mediterranean plant and likes a well-drained soil in a sunny position. Plant at a distance of 30cm (12in) apart. Cut back after flowering in early autumn to 20cm (8in) to prevent the plant becoming too woody.

CONTAINER
Hyssop looks most attractive in containers. Position in full sun and protect from cold winds and heavy frosts.

WHEN TO HARVEST
Pick the flowers as soon as they are open. You will notice that they grow in long spikes so each flower has to be teased away from the stem. Make sure you get no green parts. Preserve the flower in oils, butter or vinegars (see p138), and use sparingly.

CULINARY
The whole flower is edible and combines well with strong-flavoured dishes or where extra spice is wanted. The oil made from hyssop flowers is very good when used in French dressing and for frying onions or plain meats.

TIP
Plant hyssop in the vegetable patch, especially near cabbages, to lure white fly or, if you have a vineyard, plant near the vines to increase yield.

CHICKEN BREASTS WITH HYSSOP FLOWERS

Serves 4
2 tablespoons Dijon mustard
2 tablespoons natural yoghurt
4 chicken breasts
Freshly ground black pepper and salt
Hyssop flower oil or olive oil
4 tablespoons hyssop flowers for cooking and a further 2 dessertspoons for adding as decoration
Juice of 1 lemon
Preheat oven to 190°C, 375°F, gas mark 5

Mix the mustard and yoghurt together and coat the chicken pieces on all

sides. Sprinkle with salt and pepper.
Brush four pieces of foil with the oil
and lay one chicken breast on each.
Scatter a thick layer of flowers on
top and sprinkle with lemon juice.
Wrap the foil folding the ends tightly
so that no juices can escape. Lay
the parcels on a rack with a tray
underneath in the preheated oven for
30 minutes. Remove from the foil
packets and place on plates, scattering
the remaining flowers over the
chicken. Serve with rice or pasta and
a green herb salad.

FRENCH BEAN SALAD WITH OLIVES AND HYSSOP FLOWERS

Serves 4
450g (1lb) French beans
15 black olives, pitted
1 tablespoon hyssop leaves, chopped
2 tablespoons white and blue hyssop
flowers with greenery removed

French dressing
3 tablespoons olive oil
1 tablespoon hyssop vinegar
1 clove of garlic, crushed
Freshly ground salt and pepper

Cook the beans in boiling water for 5-7
minutes until crunchy. Drain into a
colander and revive under running
cold water. Put into a serving dish,
cover and chill in the refrigerator.
When ready to serve, stir in the black
olives, hyssop leaves and flowers.
Make the salad dressing by mixing the
ingredients together thoroughly. Pour
over the salad, toss and decorate with
a few sprigs of hyssop.

73

Lavandula angustifolia
LAVENDER

❖

Perennial, Ht. 30-90cm (1-3ft). Very aromatic blue, purple, pink or mauve spikes of flowers all summer. Long, narrow, pale greenish-grey aromatic leaves.

There is nothing more nostalgic than the smell of lavender wafting through the garden on a warm summer's day. These flowers have many uses. They are moth repellents when put into bags and added to your clothes; they make a great bath oil which helps you relax at night after the toils of the day; they are great to eat, their aromatic flavour combines well with chicken and puddings, biscuits and cakes. Look out for the tender lavenders, *L. canariensis*, *L. candicans*, *L. pinnata*, *L. dentata* and *L. viridis*, a green flowering lavender, because they all have a longer flowering season with a scent and flavour more like eucalyptus.

HOW TO GROW
SEED
Lavender can be grown from seed, but it is better to grow named species from cuttings. Seed should be sown fresh in the autumn in prepared seed or plug trays, and helped with a bottom heat of 4-10°C(40-50°F).

CUTTINGS
Take softwood cuttings from non-flowering stems in spring. Take semi-hardwood cuttings in early autumn.

WHERE TO PLANT
GARDEN
All the species need an open, sunny site in a well-drained, fertile soil. To maintain the shape of the lavender bush, trim lightly every year in spring and harder after flowering in the early autumn. Do not cut into the old wood and do not cut back if there is a threat of frost as it will damage the plant.

CONTAINER
This is an ideal method of growing lavender if you have cold wet winters. Use a well draining compost and position the container in a sunny spot. Feed throughout the flowering season with a liquid fertiliser, and in winter allow the compost nearly to dry out.

CULINARY
The flowers need to be removed from the flower head, making sure there are no green or brown bits attached. Try re-vamping some of your more tried and tested recipes using lavender sugar (see p138). Meringues and biscuits using this sugar take on a whole new perspective. Also when you barbecue use lavender oil to baste chicken pieces.

TIP
Adding six drops of lavender oil to hot bath water will help you relax after a hard day's work.

WHEN TO HARVEST
Gather the flowers just as they openand use fresh or preserve in oil, sugar or jelly (see p138).

ROAST DUCK AND LAVENDER STUFFING

Serves 6

1.5kg (3lb) duck
1 tablespoon lavender leaves (use
either green lavender or an
angustifolia), chopped
1 dessertspoon flowers (purple or
green), removed from head
50g (2oz) butter
Grated rind and juice of half a lemon
Freshly ground salt and pepper
150ml (¼ pint) stock
Preheat oven to 200°C, 400°F,
gas mark 6

Mix half the lavender leaves and half
the flowers with half the butter and
the lemon rind plus the salt and
pepper to taste.

Place this mixture inside the duck
and rub the remaining butter over
the breast of the duck.

Put the duck in a roasting tin, pour
around half of the stock and roast in
the preheated oven for 15 minutes
per 500g (1lb) and 15 minutes over.
Baste frequently.

When the duck is cooked, remove
from the roasting tin. Tip off the
excess fat from the tin, just leaving
the sediment behind. Add the
remaining stock, the lemon juice and
the remaining lavender leaves, boil
till reduced to a thick sauce and
season to taste. Strain and pour over
the duck.

Garnish with the remaining lavender
flowers plus a few extra sprigs if you
have them.

CRAB APPLE AND LAVENDER FLOWER JELLY

Makes four 450g (1lb) jars

1.75kg (4lb) crab apples
1.5kg (3lb) sugar (see recipe)
8 tablespoons lavender flowers
1 tablespoon lavender flowers for
adding to jelly

Wash and chop the crab apples, put into
a pan and add enough water just to
cover them. Bring to the boil, then
simmer for about 20 to 30 minutes until
soft and pulpy. Pour carefully into a

muslin (jelly, cheesecloth) bag and drain
into a large bowl for a day or overnight.
Measure the juice and add 450g (1lb) of
sugar to every 600ml (1 pint) of juice.
Put into a pan and bring to a rolling
boil, adding the lavender flowers tied in
a piece of muslin (cheesecloth). Cook for
about 20 minutes until setting point is
reached. At this point remove the
lavender flowers in the muslin and any
surface scum, and then add the
individual lavender flowers. Stir and
pour into warm sterilised glass jars. Seal
while still hot, and don't forget to date
and label.

Lonicera caprifolium
WILD HONEYSUCKLE

❖

Deciduous perennial creeping vine, Ht. up to 6m (20ft). The buds of this fragrant flower are pink on opening, then change to a pale white/pink/yellow.

Honeysuckle is a very nostalgic plant to me. As a child I used to pull the flowers off the plant and suck the nectar from the bottom. The sweet flavour is delightful. John Gerard's 16th-century herbal mentions that 'the flowers steeped in oil and set in the sun are good to anoint the body that is benumbed and grown very cold' – in other words it is good for circulation. *Lonicera periclymenum*, the other wild honeysuckle, has yellow flowers which are as scented and edible as *L. caprifolium* and can be used in exactly the same way.

HOW TO GROW

SEED

Sow in autumn on the surface of a pre-pared seed or plug tray. Cover with glass or plastic and winter outside. Be warned, germination can take up to two seasons.

CUTTINGS

Take cuttings from the non-flowering, semi-ripe shoots in summer and root in a bark, grit and peat mix of compost. Alternatively, take hardwood cuttings in late autumn, leaving the cuttings in a cold greenhouse for the winter.

WHERE TO PLANT

GARDEN

The extremely tolerant plant will flourish vigorously in the most unpromising of sites. Plant in autumn or spring in any fertile, well-drained soil in sun or semi-shade. The best situation is 'to put its foot in the shade and its head in the sun'. Prune in early spring and, after flowering, cut out the flowering wood or climbers.

CONTAINER

This plant can be grown in a container and lends itself to being trained into a mop-head standard. Use a bark and peat mix compost. Water regularly throughout the summer, cutting down in the winter.

WHEN TO HARVEST

When the flower is at its palest and before the nectar has been collected, it has the best flavour. These flowers can be dried, in which case, pick just as they open (see p146).

CULINARY

These sweet, heavy-perfumed flowers are lovely in fruit salads, combining well with pears, apples and grapes. A floral syrup made with the flowers (see p141) is very good, especially when poured over sweet pancakes. Equally the floral sugar (see p138) is good to use when baking cakes.

HONEYSUCKLE AND CARROT SALAD

Serves 4
250g (½lb) carrots
Pinch of sugar and salt
6 honeysuckle flowers with no green bits

Salad dressing
4 tablespoons olive oil
1 tablespoon thyme vinegar
¼ teaspoon Dijon mustard
1 small clove of garlic, crushed
Freshly ground salt and pepper

Mix the salad dressing ingredients together thoroughly. Cut the carrots into matchsticks. Put into a pan with the sugar, salt and just enough water to cover. Bring to the boil and cook un-covered for five minutes. Drain and put into a bowl; add the salad dressing, and season to taste. Chill for several hours, so the carrots absorb the dressing. Before serving, toss in the flowers.

HONEYSUCKLE BUNS

Makes 18 buns

100g (4oz) soft margarine
100g (4oz) honeysuckle sugar
(or caster sugar)
2 medium-sized eggs
100g (4oz) self-raising flour
1 teaspoon baking powder

Icing

225g (8oz) icing sugar

2-4 tablespoons hot water
90 honeysuckle flowers (5 per bun)
Preheat oven to 160°C, 325°F,
gas mark 3

Put the margarine, sugar, eggs, sifted flour and baking powder into a bowl. Mix together with a wooden spoon or electric mixer until smooth and glossy. Spoon into 18 paper cake cases or patty tins. Cook in the oven for 15 to 20 minutes until the cakes are

risen and just firm to the touch. Put them onto a wire rack to cool.

Sift the icing sugar into a bowl. Gradually beat in sufficient water to give a smooth icing, i.e. thick enough to coat the back of a spoon, adding extra water or sugar to achieve the correct consistency. Immediately spread a little of the icing over the cooled buns and sprinkle five flowers onto the icing, which will hold the flowers in place as it sets.

Mentha
MINT

❖

Perennial, Ht.15-60cm (6-24in). Tiny pink, purple, mauve and white flowers which grow in whorls or long spikes in summer. Mint-scented leaves.

Mint flowers all have a lovely, clean flavour, each unique to the species. *Mentha spicata*, spearmint, is defiantly minty, like chewing gum. *M. piperita*, peppermint, has a fruity peppermint flavour and *M. gracilis*, ginger mint, has a warm-scented flavour. Other mints with marvellous spearmint flavours are *M. spicata* 'Moroccan', Moroccan mint and *M. spicata* 'Crispa Tashkent', Tashkent mint. All can be used in salads, savoury dishes and puddings.

HOW TO GROW

SEED
Mint can be grown from seed, but the plants are inferior (in my opinion) to those produced from division and root cuttings.

DIVISION
Divide established plants every few years but be warned that each bit of root will grow. It is vital not to leave roots behind if you are moving the mint to a different part of the garden.

CUTTINGS
Root cuttings are easy. Dig up a piece of root, cut it where you can see a growing node and place the cutting in a pot, seed tray or plug tray. Water in well and place tray in a warm environment. If you do this in the spring it will take only about two weeks for the new shoots to appear.

WHERE TO PLANT

GARDEN
Plant mint with care. It can spread around your garden on its runners at an alarming rate. It prefers to be planted in sun or semi-shade and in a good soil. Having said that, mint will grow anywhere; however if the soil is very wet and a heavy clay or if it is very light then the plant may (only *may*) die out after about three seasons.

CONTAINER
Mint grows very happily in containers. Make sure the container is large enough and that the compost does not dry out. Position in semi-shade and repot every year.

WHEN TO HARVEST
Mint flowers all summer and some species into early autumn. It is best to pick and use the flowers the same day. If left in the refrigerator or frozen they seem to lose their flavour. To preserve them in butter, oil or vinegar see p138.

CULINARY
These tiny flowers really do pack a punch in flavour. They add a certain extra to green salads, fruit salads, fresh strawberries and my favourites, chocolate mousse, chocolate cake and chocolate crème.

TIP
Do not plant different varieties of mint together. In time they will lose their individual flavour, and all taste the same.

TZAZIKI WITH GINGER MINT

*½ cucumber, skinned and roughly
diced
140g (5oz) natural yoghurt
1 clove of garlic, crushed
1 tablespoon ginger mint leaves,
chopped
1 tablespoon ginger mint flowers,
removed from the flower head and
with no green attached
Freshly ground salt and pepper
4 whole ginger mint leaves and
4 whole ginger mint flowers for
decoration*

Place the cucumber in a colander,
sprinkle with salt and leave to stand
for 30 minutes to draw out the juices.
Rinse under a cold tap, drain well and
dry on absorbent kitchen towel. Put
the cucumber in a serving bowl, pour
over the yoghurt, add the garlic, mint
leaves and flowers and mix well.
Season with salt and pepper to taste.
Cover and chill in the refrigerator.
When ready to serve, decorate with
the 4 leaves and flowers.

MINT CHOCOLATE MOUSSE

Serves 4
*100g (4oz) plain dark chocolate
2 eggs, separated
1 teaspoon instant coffee granules
1 teaspoon fresh-chopped mint,
either Moroccan, spear
or Tashkent
Whipped cream and mint leaves
for decoration*

Melt the chocolate either in a
microwave or in a double saucepan.
When smooth and liquid, remove
from heat. Beat the egg yolks and
add to the chocolate while hot (this
will cook the yolks slightly), then mix
in the coffee and chopped mint. Leave
to cool for about 15 minutes. Beat the
egg whites (not too stiff) and fold them
into the cooling chocolate mixture with
a metal spoon. Pour into containers,
decorate with cream and garnish.

Monarda didyma
BERGAMOT, BEE BALM

❖

Perennial, Ht. 45cm (18in). Fantastic red, pink, white or
purple flowers throughout the summer. Aromatic leaves.

The flamboyant flower of the bergamot will enhance any herb garden or
perennial border. It has a distinctive fragrant and spicy scent which totally
conceals the powerful flavour of the flower - a combination of spice, thyme
and mint. Use the petals sparingly in salads, vegetable dishes, pasta and
strong-flavoured fish. There are many cultivars and varieties of bergamot
worth looking out for *Monarda* 'Croftway Pink', bergamot 'Croftway
Pink', which has a beautiful pink flower and *M. fistulosa*, wild bergamot,
has a delicate mauve flower and the strongest flavour of all the bergamots.

HOW TO GROW
SEED
Only the species will grow true
from seed. Sow the small seed in
spring under protection in a seed
or plug tray. It will need temperatures
of 21°C (65°F) to germinate. Plant
out only when the soil has begun
to warm and there is no threat
of frost.

CUTTINGS
This is the best method to propagate
cultivars and should be done after
the early summer growth when the
shoots are 7.5-10cm (3-4in) long.

DIVISION
Divide established plants (around
three years old) in early spring.
Replant in the garden in a well
prepared site which has had a good
amount of rotted compost dug in.
Plant at a distance of 45cm (18in)
from other plants.

WHERE TO PLANT
GARDEN
All the bergamots grow well in moist,
nutrient-rich soil, preferably in a
semi-shaded spot; deciduous
woodland is ideal. They do not like
clay soils. In autumn it is a good idea
to cut the plants back to the ground
and give them a good feed with manure
or compost.

CONTAINER
Despite the height of this plant it can
look most attractive in a large
container (35-45 cm/14-18in in
diameter). Make sure that the
container is placed in semi-shade and
don't let the soil dry out completely.

WHEN TO HARVEST
Cut the flowers as soon as they are
fully opened. They can be used fresh
or dried. They dry beautifully and
keep their colour (see p146). Keep the
petals in an air-tight, dark jar, which
will keep the flavour for about three
months. You can also preserve them in
oil or vinegar (see p142).

CULINARY
The bergamot flower can be very
strongly flavoured, especially the
Monarda fistulosa, wild bergamot, so
check first before adding too much to
your dishes. The robust flavour
complements pork dishes, fish and
chicken. The following recipe can be
adapted for any strongly flavoured
white fish.

TIP
Slugs are a real pest to all varieties of
bergamot so be on your guard,
particularly in spring.

COD STEAKS WITH BERGAMOT

Serves 4

4 cod steaks (or halibut)
40g (1½oz) butter
1 tablespoon olive oil
1 tablespoon bergamot leaves,
chopped
1 dessertspoon plain flour
1 tablespoon bergamot flowers for
sauce and a few extra for
decoration, removed from the main
head and no green bits attached
150ml (5fl oz) white wine

Rinse the cod steaks and pat dry. Melt the butter and olive oil in a large frying pan. Add the cod steaks and the bergamot leaves and flowers. Cook on each side for five minutes over a moderate heat until lightly browned. Remove the steaks from the pan and put them in a warmed serving dish. Add the flour to the juices left in the pan, mix well for one minute then add the white wine, stirring well to prevent any lumps developing. Bring to the boil, and cook for two minutes. Pour over the fish, adding extra flowers for decoration.

BERGAMOT AND BURGHUL SALAD

Serves 4-6

100g (4oz) burghul (crushed wheat)
2 bunches spring onions, chopped
225g (8oz) tomatoes, skinned and
chopped
1 dessertspoon bergamot flowers with
no green attached
1 teaspoon bergamot leaves, chopped
4 tablespoons olive oil
3 tablespoons lemon juice
Salt and freshly ground black pepper
1 whole bergamot flower for
decoration

Soak the burghul for 30 minutes in cold water, then drain and squeeze dry, using your hands. Place in a bowl, add the spring onions, tomatoes and bergamot leaves and flowers, stir well then add the oil and lemon juice, and mix well. Season to taste with salt and pepper. Decorate with a complete bergamot flower in the centre. This can be served as a first course or as a light main meal with hot bread rolls.

Myrrhis odorata
SWEET CICELY

❖

Perennial, Ht. 60-90cm (2-3ft). Small, white, sweet-scented flowers in large umbels from spring to early summer. The fern-like leaves smell and taste of aniseed.

Sweet cicely has a long reputation as the sugar herb because the leaves have a very high saccharine content. Both the flowers and leaves have a sweet anise flavour and combine well with many different fruit dishes such as gooseberries, plums and rhubarb. They also make a very good wine.

HOW TO GROW

SEED

Sow the large seed when it ripens in early autumn into prepared seed or plug trays, putting in only one seed per plug. The seed requires several months of cold winter temperatures in order to germinate. Check that the compost does not dry out during the winter and also that the mice have not feasted on the seed.

DIVISION

Divide established roots in autumn.

CUTTINGS

Take root cuttings in the spring or autumn.

WHERE TO PLANT

GARDEN

Sweet cicely is a native of Europe and it can be invasive in certain soil conditions, so if your soil is light and poor, beware. Otherwise, plant in a soil that is rich in humus and position in light shade. Sweet cicely does not grow successfully in humid areas.

CONTAINER

Sweet cicely has a long tap root, so make sure the container you use is large. Place the container in semi-shade and do not let the soil dry out during the growing season.

WHEN TO HARVEST

Pick the flowers young and fresh, preserve either in sugar or syrup, or make a jelly from them (see p138).

CULINARY

The whole of the small sweet cicely flower is edible. Remove each flower from the cluster, making sure all green bits are removed. The sweet anise flavour is lovely with tart fruit dishes; try it mixed with apple purée, plum fool or rhubarb tart.

TIP

As this is one of the first nectar plants to appear in the garden it is valuable for the bees.

SWEET CICELY AND REDCURRANT SNOW

Serves 4

150ml (¼ pint) whipping cream
2 egg whites
150ml (¼ pint) natural yoghurt
2 tablespoons caster sugar
450g (1lb) redcurrants
1 tablespoon sweet cicely leaves, finely chopped
2 tablespoons sweet cicely flowers

Whip the cream until thick and beat the egg whites until stiff but not dry. Beat the yoghurt until smooth. Mix the egg whites into the cream, followed by the yoghurt, folding both in lightly. Stir in the sugar. Wash and drain the redcurrants, making sure there are no stalks still attached. Stir into the mixture, adding the sweet cicely leaves and half the flowers. Pour into a serving dish, and decorate with the remaining flowers.

STRAWBERRIES AND SWEET CICELY FLOWERS

Serves 4

450g (1lb) fresh strawberries, washed and hulled
Caster sugar to taste (optional)
1 tablespoon sweet cicely flowers

Put the fresh strawberries in a serving bowl. Add sugar to taste. Scatter the sweet cicely flowers over. Chill in the refrigerator before serving.

Myrtus communis

MYRTLE

❖

Tender, evergreen perennial, Ht. 2-3m (6-10ft). Fragrant white flowers from spring until midsummer. Small, dark green, aromatic oval leaves.

These beautiful fragrant flowers, traditionally carried by the bride in her bouquet, have a delightfully spicy, warm-scented flavour which combines well with light meats and strong fish dishes. They also make an interesting addition to fruit dishes. All the flowers of *Myrtus communis* 'Variegata', variegated myrtle, *M. communis* ssp. *tarentina*, myrtle tarentina, and *M. communis* Tarentina 'Variegata', variegated myrtle tarentina, are edible and have the same flavour as the true *Myrtus communis*.

HOW TO GROW

SEED

Myrtle does not grow successfully from seed in the English climate, needing higher temperatures to do well. Sow the seed in spring in prepared seed or plug trays. When large enough either pot up and grow on or, if the climate is warm enough, plant out. Protect for the first few winters.

CUTTINGS

Take softwood cuttings in spring. Once rooted, pot up and grow on for two years in England before planting out in the garden.

WHERE TO PLANT

GARDEN

Plant in fertile, well-drained soil in full sun. Protect in winter if you have any degree of frost. Dig up and bring into a cold greenhouse if your winter temperatures fall below -2°C (28°F) and replant the following spring.

CONTAINER

In cold climates myrtle is well suited to growing in containers and it looks most attractive. Position the container in the garden in full sun. Water well in summer, but keep on the dry side in winter. Bring into a cold greenhouse if necessary.

WHEN TO HARVEST

Pick the flowers when they are newly opened and use fresh, or preserve the petals in sugar or crystallise the whole flower (see p138).

CULINARY

The only truly edible bits of this flower are the petals. Crystallise the whole flower, which looks lovely and can be used to decorate cakes and puddings.

TIP

In the language of flowers, myrtle is the symbol of love and constancy. For this reason every bride should carry a sprig of myrtle in her bouquet on her wedding day.

MYRTLE FLOWERS WITH PORK LOIN CHOPS

Serves 8

15g (½oz) butter
1 tablespoon sunflower oil
1 large onion, finely sliced
1 clove of garlic, crushed
8 pork loin chops
30g (1oz) plain flour
300ml (½ pint) white wine
1 teaspoon myrtle leaves, finely chopped
1 tablespoon myrtle flower petals
6 whole myrtle flowers for garnish
Preheat oven to 180°C, 350°F, gas mark 4

Melt the butter in the oil in a large frying pan, add the onion and garlic, and cook until translucent. Remove from the pan, leaving the fat, and set aside. In the same fat, lightly brown the pork chops on both sides for four to five minutes. Place in an ovenproof dish with a lid and keep warm. Mix flour into the pan juices and cook over a low heat for at least one minute until it is completely absorbed. Add the wine, stirring all the time, and bring to the boil. Add the myrtle leaves, onions and garlic and simmer for a further two minutes. Pour over the pork chops, cover and bake in the oven for 25 minutes. Remove from the oven and arrange the meat in a serving dish. Remove any excess fat from the sauce, stir and pour over the chops. Scatter over the myrtle petals and whole flowers. Serve with a dish of mashed potato and fresh green broccoli.

AVOCADO AND MYRTLE

Serves 4

2 ripe avocados
1 green lettuce
2 beef tomatoes
4 whole myrtle flowers
1 tablespoon myrtle petals

French dressing
3 tablespoons thyme oil (or olive oil)
1 tablespoon white wine vinegar
½ teaspoon myrtle leaves, finely chopped
salt and pepper

Slice the avocados in half, peel and pit. Arrange the lettuce leaves on four individual plates and then half an avocado, cut side up. Skin the tomatoes and slice thinly, cut into half slices and place around each avocado. Make the French dressing by mixing the oil and vinegar together and add the half teaspoon of finely chopped myrtle leaves. Season. Dribble a little dressing into the cavity of each of avocado half and place a whole flower in each. Dribble a small amount of dressing over the tomatoes, then scatter the petals over the tomatoes.

Nepeta cataria
CATMINT

❖

Perennial, Ht. 45cm-1m (18in-3ft). White to pale pink flowers from early summer to early autumn. Pungent, aromatic, green leaves with serrated edges.

Catmint or catnep is synonymous with cats because they are forever eating it and then lolling around feeling high. This will not happen to you, I might hasten to add, when you eat the small flowers. They have an aromatic mint/spice flavour and are quite strong, so do not go mad when using them in cooking. They combine well with pasta, rice and vegetables of all sorts, adding an extra bite. The flowers of *Nepeta x faassenii*, *Nepeta racemosa*, both of which have blue flowers, and *Nepeta cataria* 'Citriodora', lemon catmint, which has a creamy pink flower, are all edible, each with subtly different flavours. The lemon catmint certainly does have a mint/thyme/lemon flavour and complements fish dishes.

HOW TO GROW

SEED

Sow the small seed in spring or late summer into prepared seed or plug trays. A bottom heat of 15-21°C (60-70°F) will assist germination.

DIVISION

Divide established plants in early autumn. Beware of being invaded by your cat or your neighbour's cat when you do this, because the bruised roots will draw them in, as they cannot resist the smell.

CUTTINGS

Take softwood cuttings from the non-flowering tips of the new growth in late spring until early summer.

WHERE TO PLANT

GARDEN

All the nepetas like a well-drained soil in full sun or light shade. They dislike being wet in winter and are known to rot off if it is excessively wet. Plant at a distance of 50cm (20in) from other plants.

CONTAINER

The blue flowering *N. x faassenii* and *N. racemosa* look most attractive in terracotta pots. Always cut back after flowering. Position the pot in sun or partial shade.

WHEN TO HARVEST

Use the small flowers fresh or preserve in oils or vinegars (see p142). They also can make a good jelly (see p138) which goes well with meat dishes, especially lamb.

CULINARY

The whole flower is edible. When preparing the flowers for use in a recipe, remove any green bits, otherwise the flavour will be impaired. The leaves and stem have a more powerful flavour.

TIP

The dried leaves stuffed into a toy mouse will keep kittens and cats amused for hours.

CATMINT FLOWER BISCUITS

The spicy mint flavour of these biscuits may well cause a surprise when offered to an unsuspecting guest.

Makes about 14 biscuits
100g (4oz) butter
50g (2oz) caster sugar
175g (6oz) self-raising flour
Pinch of salt
1 tablespoon catmint flowers, divided into individual florets
Preheat oven to 230°C, 450°F, gas mark 7
Use a 7.5cm (3in) cutter

Cream the sugar and butter together until light and fluffy, fold in the flour and salt. Knead into a dough. Roll out and scatter the flowers over the dough and lightly roll in. Make into any shape of your choice with a cutter. Place on a greased baking sheet. Bake for 10-12 minutes. Cool on a wire tray.

POTATO SALAD WITH PINK AND BLUE CATMINT FLOWERS

Serves 4
900g (2lb) potatoes
300ml (½ pint) mayonnaise
2 tablespoons mixed catmint flowers, divided into individual florets

Peel the potatoes and cut into chunks. Put into a pan of boiling water and cook for 10-15 minutes, until firm but not raw. Drain and cool. Cut up into small chunks. As bought mayonnaise now tastes very good I suggest you use your favourite brand. Empty sufficient into a bowl and stir in one tablespoon of mixed catmint flowers. Add the potatoes and coat thoroughly. Cover and chill in the refrigerator for at least one hour. Before serving, remove from the refrigerator, scatter on the remaining catmint flowers.

Ocimum basilicum
BASIL

❖

Tender annual, Ht. 23-45cm (9-18in). Purple, pink and white
flowers in summer. Highly aromatic leaves of green and purple.

This herb grows and grows in popularity. There are many varieties, from
Ocimum basilicum 'Cinnamon', cinnamon basil, *O. basilicum* var.
citriodorum, lemon basil, *O. basilicum* 'Napolitano', lettuce leaved basil, to
a special culinary basil from Thailand, *Ocimum* 'Horapha', Horapha basil,
(Rau Que) and there are many more to look out for. To promote leaf growth,
pick off the flowers, which have the same delightful flavour as the leaves; to
add a cinnamon taste to your dish simply add cinnamon basil flowers etc. In
general the flowers have a milder flavour than the leaves but still enhance
tomato dishes, rice, pasta dishes, chicken, fish and vegetable dishes.

Water well at midday but do not
over-water.

HOW TO GROW

SEED

Do not be in a hurry to sow this herb,
even a small fluctuation in
temperature from day to night can
make the young seedlings 'damp off'.
So wait until the temperatures are
levelling out; late spring is ideal. Sow
on the surface of a prepared plug tray

or seed tray, keep the watering to the
minimum and never after midday.
Basil is the most cantankerous man
you could wish to meet, he simply
hates going to bed wet.

WHERE TO PLANT

GARDEN

Sow direct into the garden only when
the evening temperatures do not drop
below 13°C (55°F). Make sure that the
site is well prepared and that the till is
as fine as possible. The soil needs to be
rich and well drained and the situation
warm and sheltered, preferably with
sun at midday.

CONTAINER

Basil will happily grow in containers
placed on the kitchen window sill or in
pots by the back door in full sun. In
Southern Europe basil is placed in
pots outside houses to repel flies.

WHEN TO HARVEST

You will find that there is a small but
continuous supply of flowers if you
keep picking the flowers off basil to
promote new leaf growth. They do
not freeze and are not worth drying.
I recommend making floral oils
and vinegars (see p142) which are
lovely used in salad dressings and
stir-fry dishes.

CULINARY

These flowers combine well with
different dishes, for example lemon
basil flowers in a tuna fish salad, or
Thai basil flowers with stir-fried pork.
If you want the basil flavour uncluttered
by other foods try the following recipes.

TIP

Rub crushed basil leaves onto your
skin as an excellent mosquito
repellent.

BASIL FLOWERS WITH TOMATO AND MOZZARELLA SALAD

Serves 3-4

450g (1lb) large beef tomatoes
225g (8oz) mozzarella cheese
Freshly ground black pepper and salt
1 tablespoon white wine vinegar
3 tablespoons basil oil
6 basil leaves finely chopped
2 tablespoon basil flowers (lemon,
sweet or Greek basil)
6 black olives, pitted

Skin the tomatoes and slice thinly. Lay them in one half of the serving dish. Thinly slice the cheese and put on the other half of the dish. Season. Mix the vinegar and oil together and pour over. Scatter the whole dish with the basil leaves and flowers. Garnish with olives.

CREME FRAICHE WITH PURPLE BASIL

1 small carton crème fraîche
10 purple basil leaves, chopped
1 tablespoon purple basil flowers
1 iceberg lettuce

Mix the small carton of crème fraîche with the purple basil leaves and flowers. Place this mixture in the centre of a leaf of iceberg lettuce so that it is like a small dish. This mixture can be used as a dip or a filling for jacket potatoes.

PESTO SAUCE

Serves 4

1 tablespoon pine nuts
4 tablespoons chopped basil leaves
2 cloves garlic, chopped
6 tablespoons olive oil
75g (3oz) grated parmesan cheese
salt and freshly ground pepper
1 tablespoon basil flowers

Blend the pine nuts, basil leaves and garlic until smooth. Slowly add the oil, blend until you have a thick paste. Add the cheese and season to taste. Stir in the flowers, saving a few for decoration.

Oenothera biennis
EVENING PRIMROSE

❖

Hardy biennial, Ht. 90-120cm (3-4ft). Large, evening-scented, yellow flowers for most of the summer. Long, green, oval or lance-shaped leaves.

These fluorescent yellow flowers, which can lighten the evening air with their gentle perfume, do not do justice to themselves with their flavour which is similar to lettuce. Having said that, they do decorate salads, cream cheese, cucumber and all mild flavoured foods. Another evening primrose worth cultivating is the low-growing *Oenothera macrocarpa*, but beware - only the petals of this variety are edible.

HOW TO GROW

SEED

Carefully sow the very fine seed in early spring on the surface of prepared pots or plug trays. When all threat of frost has gone, plant out at a distance of 30cm (12in) apart.

WHERE TO PLANT

GARDEN

Evening primrose will grow in practically any soil, but if given a choice it prefers a well-drained soil in a dry, sunny corner. A timely warning: this plant does self-seed which can be annoying.

CONTAINER

As *Oenothera macrocarpa* is low growing it looks excellent in containers and combines well with other plants, giving a good show in window boxes or tubs.

WHEN TO HARVEST

Pick the whole spike with the flowers attached and place in water until needed. These flowers close very quickly so place the vase with the spikes in full sun. Use them fresh. They are difficult to preserve, but, as they are prolific flowerers, you should have a good supply for a large part of the growing season.

CULINARY

The whole flower of *Oenothera biennis* is edible, once all the green has been removed. Like the day lily (see p68), it can be used in bud or in full flower. The lettuce flavour goes well with many dishes and the yellow flower combines beautifully with a green salad.

TIP

The young leaves and the roots are also edible. The roots taste like sweet parsnips, so if you have a mass invasion do not despair.

BUTTERED BROAD BEANS WITH EVENING PRIMROSE FLOWERS

Serves 4

450g (1lb) baby broad beans
50g (2oz) butter
1 teaspoon lemon juice
Salt and freshly ground black pepper
1 tablespoon evening primrose petals
6 evening primrose flowers, whole,
with green bits removed

As the broad beans are going to be cooked in their pods they must be very young and the pods thin and not more than 10-13cm (4-5in) long. Top and tail them and cut each diagonally into three or four pieces. Place in a colander and wash under cold water. Bring a large pan of water to the boil and place the drained beans into the pan. Bring back to the boil and cook for eight minutes or until tender, then drain.

Return the empty pan to the heat and add the butter, followed by the broad beans. Toss, adding the lemon juice and seasoning. Add the flower petals and turn into a serving dish. Decorate with the 6 whole evening primroses and serve.

CUCUMBER, MINT AND FROMAGE FRAIS WITH EVENING PRIMROSE FLOWERS

Serves 4-6

2 large cucumbers
Salt
125ml (¼ pint) fromage frais
3 tablespoons spearmint (either Moroccan or Tashkent), chopped
6 evening primrose buds, sliced
6 whole evening primrose flowers, with green bits removed

Cut one cucumber into small dice. Peel the other and cut into finger-length pieces. Put all the cucumber pieces into a large colander and sprinkle with salt. Leave for at least 30 minutes, then rinse under the cold tap and pat dry in kitchen towel. In a bowl, mix the fromage frais with the mint, the diced cucumber and the sliced evening primrose buds. Put this mixture into a serving bowl, cover and chill. To serve, decorate with the finger-size pieces of cucumber and the whole evening primrose flowers.

Origanum vulgare
OREGANO

❖

Perennial, Ht. 23-45cm (9-18in). Cluster of tiny, tubular, mauve, pink or white flowers in summer. Dark-green, aromatic, slightly hairy leaves.

The flowers of oregano and marjoram are similar yet they each have a unique flavour, all depending on the species. For example, *Origanum marjorana*, sweet marjoram, has tiny white flowers which have a warm spicy sweet flavour. *Origanum* ssp. *hirtum*, Greek oregano, also has small white flowers but they pack quite a punch in flavour, hot and spicy, so you need only small amounts. *Origanum vulgare* 'Aureum', golden oregano, has pink flowers with a warm spicy flavour. The flowers of all oreganos combine well with chicken, fish and vegetable dishes. They also make great floral oils and vinegars, which is the ideal way to preserve them.

HOW TO GROW

SEED
Sow the very fine seed in spring into prepared seed or plug trays. Do not cover with compost or perlite. Use a bottom heat of 15°C (60°F) to help germination. Keep watering to the minimum when the seedlings are young.

CUTTINGS
Take softwood cuttings from the new growth in spring.

DIVISION
Divide established plants in the spring or early autumn. Replant where required.

WHERE TO PLANT

GARDEN
Plant both oregano and marjoram in a sunny position in a well-drained soil. The exception is golden oregano appreciates a bit of shade to stop the leaves from scorching.

CONTAINER
All *Origanum* species look attractive in containers. Use a well-drained compost and do not over water. Cut back after flowering in order to encourage new growth.

WHEN TO HARVEST
Pick the small flowers just as they open and preserve in oil, vinegar, or butter (see p138).

CULINARY
These small flowers have a strong flavour so use them sparingly. The whole flower is edible once removed from its growing socket; make sure no green bits remain. The following two recipes show how versatile these flowers can be.

TIP
Make an infusion from the leaves and add it to your bath to ease tired muscles and backache.

MARINATED TROUT WITH GREEK OREGANO FLOWERS

Serves 4
8 trout fillets, or 2 whole trout with the heads and tails removed

Marinade
300ml (½ pint) dry white wine
4 tablespoons oregano flower vinegar
1 shallot
1 carrot
1 clove of garlic
1 bay leaf
6 black peppercorns
3 sprigs French parsley
2 sprigs Greek oregano

Sour cream sauce
6 tablespoons sour cream or
crème fraîche
Pinch of dry mustard
Freshly ground black pepper
Sea salt

Finishing touch
2 tablespoons pink oregano flowers

Place the trout in a lidded frying
pan or ovenproof dish. Put all the
ingredients for the marinade into a
small saucepan and bring to the
boil. Simmer for 20 minutes and
then pour over the trout. Simmer
for a further 10 minutes and then
leave the fish to cool in the marinade.

When cool, remove the trout, strain
the remaining marinade and reserve
for the sauce. If using whole fish,
skin and bone and cut into eight
fillets.

Arrange in a shallow serving dish.
Put the sour cream in a bowl and
mix it with a pinch of mustard
and two tablespoons of the strained
marinade. Season to taste with salt
and pepper. Beat until smooth and
pour over the fillets.

Finally scatter the two tablespoons of
oregano flowers over the fillets in the
sauce. Serve as a first course.

BABY BEETROOT IN WHITE SAUCE WITH MARJORAM

Serves 4-6
8 whole baby beetroot

White sauce
30g (1oz) butter
30g (1oz) flour
30g (1oz) flour
1 tablespoon marjoram flowers (in
individual florets with no green bits)
300 ml (½ pint) milk
Salt and freshly ground black pepper
Extra marjoram flowers

Prepare the beetroot by cutting off the
tops, leaving about 2cm (1in) of stem.
Wash them in cold water taking care
not to pierce the skin, otherwise the
beetroots will 'bleed' in cooking. Put

into a pan of boiling water and cook
for 30-45 minutes. To see if they are
ready, lift from the pan and press with
your fingers; if the skin slips off easily,
the beetroot is cooked. Strain and cool
before peeling.

Make the white sauce by melting the
butter and adding the flour. Cook for
one minute then add the marjoram
flowers and milk, stirring all the time.
Cook until the sauce becomes thick
and smooth, season and pour over the
beetroot. Put in the oven at 180ºC,
350ºF or gas 4 for 10 minutes. Before
serving, garnish with more flowers.

Perilla frutescens var. *crispa*
PERILLA - SHISO - JAPANESE BASIL

❖

Annual, Ht. 60cm-1.2m (2-4ft). Small, white flowers in summer. Slightly crinkled, green, aromatic leaves.

I started growing this plant over ten years ago for culinary use and was recently amazed to find it happily growing in bedding displays throughout England. It is a very striking plant and the small flowers have a lovely, sweet, light, spicy flavour which complements stir-fry dishes, chicken and fish. *Perilla frutescens* var. *crispa rubra*, purple shiso, has small pink flowers which have the same flavour. The combination of purple leaves and pink flowers is irresistible in lots of culinary dishes.

HOW TO GROW

SEED
Sow the seeds in spring into prepared seed or plug trays. Germination can be erratic, a bottom heat of 18°C (65°F) being helpful if you want to start the seeds in early spring.

WHERE TO PLANT
Sow direct into the garden only when the evening temperatures do not drop below 10°C (50°F). Make sure the site is well prepared and the till is as fine as possible. The soil needs to be rich and well drained and the position warm and sheltered, preferably with sun at midday.

CONTAINER
Shiso will happily grow in containers placed on the kitchen window sill or by the back door if in full sun. Keep potting on the plant as it grows; it will grow large, so be warned. To prevent it becoming too tall, pinch out the growing tip, which will also

help leaf and flower production. Water well at midday but do not drown.

WHEN TO HARVEST
Keep picking the flowers to promote new leaf growth and you will find that there is a small but continuous supply. They are best preserved in a floral oil or vinegar (see p142) which adds subtle flavour to salad dressings and stir-fry dishes.

CULINARY
The whole flower can be eaten. Experiment with them; they are versatile and dramatic. Here are two recipes to whet your appetite.

TIP
The leaves of the purple shiso can be used to colour preserved fruits.

SHISO AND RICOTTA RAMEKINS

Serves 6
Enough purple shiso leaves to line six ramekins (this will require approx. 24 leaves depending on the size)
140g (5oz) ricotta cheese
140g (5oz) fromage frais
75g (2½oz) butter, softened
2 cloves of garlic, crushed
Salt and freshly ground black pepper
2 tablespoons shiso flowers

First line the ramekin dishes with cling film, leaving enough hanging over the side so that the dish can be covered when put in the refrigerator.
    Line each dish with the leaves, again leaving an overhang. Ensure that you have enough leaves left over to cover the top. If the leaves are on the older side of young, it is a good idea to dip each leaf into a bowl of very hot water for a few seconds before lining the dish, to

soften the leaf and make it easier to mould.

Mix thoroughly the ricotta, fromage frais, butter and garlic. Add the salt and pepper and half the shiso flowers and then mix again. Put this mixture into the lined moulds, cover with the remaining shiso leaves and then finally with the cling film. Put in the refrigerator overnight.

Before serving unwrap the top of the cling film, turn the ramekin upside down on the serving plate and remove the rest of the cling film. Decorate each with the remaining shiso flowers.

Serve either as a salad or as first course with toast.

CHICKEN, RICE AND PINE NUTS WRAPPED IN SHISO LEAVES

Serves 4

Oil for frying
1 small onion, finely chopped
100g (4oz) rice, cooked
100g (4oz) chicken, cooked and diced
1 tablespoon pine nuts
1 teaspoon tarragon, finely chopped
1 teaspoon thyme, finely chopped
1 tablespoon shiso flowers
16 shiso leaves

Heat the oil in a large frying pan and cook the onion until soft and translucent. Add the rice, chicken, pine nuts, tarragon, thyme and two

teaspoons of shiso flowers. Mix altogether and cook for 2 minutes, then remove from the heat.

Prepare the shiso leaves by putting some boiling water into a bowl and dipping each leaf in turn into the very hot water and then placing it flat on a board. Into eight of the leaves, place a teaspoon of the mixture. Roll the leaf up like a cigar. Lay out the remaining eight leaves. Onto each put one stuffed leaf and roll the other way. This will seal the 'cigars' and keep the stuffing in place. Arrange on a serving plate, cover and chill in a refrigerator.

When ready to serve, scatter the remaining flowers over the shiso leaves as decoration. Serve as a first course with a vinaigrette.

Pelargonium
SCENTED GERANIUMS
❖

Tender perennial, Ht. 30cm-1m (1-3ft). There are many different varieties of scented geranium. The common name is a botanical misnomer but for clarity I will use it to stop any confusion with the large Pelargonium family. They flower in summer and are of varying colour and size. The aromatic leaves also vary in shape from deeply serrated to rounded and lobed. The scent of the leaf varies from lemon and rose, peppermint to spice.

Although it is the scented leaf of these geraniums that one initially notices, some of the flowers are very good to eat. For example, *Pelargonium* 'Attar of Roses' has delicate pink flowers, *Pelargonium crispum* has small pink flowers and *Pelargonium* 'Royal Oak', has large pink-purple flowers with deeper coloured flashes. The flowers of *Pelargonium* 'Lemon Fancy' are pink with a dark pink flash, *Pelargonium* 'Mable Grey's' flowers are mauve with deeper veining in summer, whereas *Pelargonium odoratissimum* and *Pelargonium fragrans* have delicate white flowers. This list is endless, all are edible and, although not of spectacular flavour in comparison to the leaf, they certainly can complement many dishes.

HOW TO GROW
SEED
Scented geraniums can be grown from seed by sowing in prepared seed or plug trays in spring with a minimum bottom heat of 15°C (60°F). For the majority of scented geraniums it is much more reliable to take cuttings.

CUTTINGS
Take softwood cuttings in summer from non-flowering shoots and insert into plug trays or small pots. These should be placed in a cool greenhouse or cool conservatory for the winter, keeping the compost dry and watering only very occasionally. In the spring re-pot into larger pots and water sparingly until they start to grow.

WHERE TO PLANT
GARDEN
Plant out in the garden as soon as there is no danger of frost. Choose a warm site with well-drained soil. If you live in a frost-prone area, lift the plants in late summer or early autumn, pot up and over-winter in a cool greenhouse.

CONTAINER
Scented geraniums make marvellous pot plants and I think this is the best way of growing them. It also makes it easy to control the environment in which these tender perennials are growing. If possible place them in a position where you can rub the leaves in passing and pick the flowers when needed.

WHEN TO HARVEST
Pick the flowers when they first open. It is only the petals that are used in cooking, although you can use the whole flower as a garnish. The best way to preserve them is in jelly, oil, butter or syrup (see p138).

CULINARY
Scented geraniums were used extensively by the Victorians to flavour food and are now returning to fashion.

TIP
Scented geranium oil is used in aromatherapy as a relaxant. Dilute one drop of scented geranium oil to two teaspoons of almond oil to treat dry skin.

'ATTAR OF ROSES' JELLY

**The following quantities should fill
four 450g (1lb) jars**
1.75 kg (4lb) cooking apples
1.75 litres (3 pints) water
1kg (2lb) sugar
12 complete scented geranium flowers
12 Pelargonium 'Attar of Roses' leaves
4 tablespoons lemon juice
*The petals from 12 scented geranium
flowers for adding at the end*

Wash and chop the apples, cores
and all, and put into a large pan
with a lid. Add all the water and
bring to the boil. Simmer until the
apples become soft and pulpy, which
takes anything from 20-30 minutes
depending on the variety of apple.
Pour carefully into a muslin (jelly,
cheesecloth) bag. Leave to drain
over a bowl all day or overnight.

Measure the juice into a pan and
add 450g (1lb) of sugar to every
600ml (1 pint) of juice. Bring to the
boil, adding the flowers and leaves tied
in a piece of muslin or cheesecloth.
Boil for about 20 minutes until setting
point is reached. Test by dropping a
little onto a cold saucer. If the surface
wrinkles when you push it with your
finger, it is ready. Remove the flowers
and leaves and the surface scum, stir
in the lemon juice and the petals from
12 flowers and pour into warmed jars.
Seal when cool, date and label.

LEMON PELARGONIUM
BISCUITS

For this recipe choose any of the
lemon-scented varieties, for example
P. 'Mable Grey' or P. 'Lemon Fancy'

Makes about 30 biscuits
225g (8oz) self-raising flour
Pinch of salt
150g (6oz) butter
100g (4oz) caster sugar
*1 teaspoon lemon-scented geranium
leaves, finely chopped*
1 egg
*Petals from 30 lemon-scented
geranium flowers*
Preheat oven to 180°C, 350°F,
gas mark 4

Sift the flour and salt into a bowl, then
rub in the butter to breadcrumb
consistency. Add the sugar, chopped
leaves and egg and mix to a very stiff
dough. Remove from the bowl, knead
until smooth, wrap in cling film or foil
and chill for 30-40 minutes. On a
lightly floured surface roll the dough
out fairly thinly and cut, using a round
5cm (2in) cutter or other shape of your
choice. Place on a baking tray lined
with non-stick parchment or
greaseproof paper. Prick the biscuits
well with a fork. Cook in the oven for
12-15 minutes until pale gold. As you
remove the biscuits from the heat,
place two or three petals from the
flowers onto each biscuit before they
harden. Place on a wire rack to cool
and store in an airtight tin.

Phlox drummondii
PHLOX
❖

Annual, Ht. 15cm (6in). Star-shaped flowers in many colours
including red, pink, blue, purple and white from summer until
early autumn. Lance-shaped pale-green leaves.

The flowers have a slightly scented flavour and are lovely in salads or
crystallised as a garnish for puddings. There are also many perennial plants
of this genus, some of which are evergreen. One which is becoming rare and
certainly worth growing is *Phlox paniculata* 'Album', ht.1.2m (4ft), but
only the white flower petals of this perennial are edible.

HOW TO GROW
SEED
Sow the seed into prepared seed or
plug trays in autumn. Winter in a
cold greenhouse and plant out in
the spring when the frosts have
gone. To produce later flowering
plants, sow in the spring direct
into the ground after frosts are
over. Thin to a distance of 10cm
(4in) apart.

CUTTINGS
Perennial varieties only work this
way. Take softwood cuttings from
non-flowering shoots in spring or
early summer.

WHERE TO PLANT
GARDEN
Plant in sun or semi-shade in
fertile, moist but well-drained soil.
If the weather is dry and hot in
summer it is a good idea to provide
the plants with some extra mulch to
help them retain moisture and also
additional watering.

CONTAINER
There are quite a few alpine varieties
of phlox such as *Phlox hoodii*, *Phlox*
'Millstream', and *Phlox* 'May Snow',
which look lovely in shallow alpine
containers as long as you have a
very, very well-drained compost.

WHEN TO HARVEST
Pick the flowers when they just
open and use fresh or preserve
by crystallising (see p142).

CULINARY
These attractive flowers are a great
addition either to a floral salad or
to any pudding. Carefully remove
the stamen and pistils from the
flower and any greenery that may
be attached before using.

TIP
Keep dead-heading the flowers to
promote new growth.

PEARS IN RED WINE DECORATED WITH WHITE PHLOX FLOWERS

Serves 6
145g (5oz) granulated sugar
150ml (¼ pint) water
150ml (¼ pint) red wine
Strips of lemon rind
Small stick of cinnamon
6 ripe eating pears
1 teaspoon arrowroot
12 white phlox flowers, crystallised

Make the syrup by dissolving the sugar
in the water, stirring continually so
that the sugar does not stick to the
bottom of the pan. Add the wine,
lemon rind and cinnamon, and, still
stirring, bring to the boil and cook for
one minute. Remove from the heat.
Peel the pears, keeping the stalks and
the eye in the base of each pear. Place
them in a pan, pour over the syrup
and poach, covered, over a gentle heat
until tender. Be patient: it takes about
25 minutes, even with ripe pears. If

you hurry the pears will discolour around the core. Once cooked, remove the pears and arrange them on a serving dish. Reduce the syrup by half by simmering. Mix the arrowroot in a little water and add to the syrup. Bring back to the boil and cook until the syrup clears, stirring continuously. Spoon over the pears and chill. Decorate with the crystallised white phlox flowers.

SUGARED WHITE PHLOX WITH WATERMELON GRANITA

Serves 4

125g (4½oz) caster sugar
250ml (9fl oz) water
2kg (4lb) watermelon (this should give approximately 1kg/2lb of flesh)
Juice of 1 lemon
Caster sugar and whipped egg white for frosting the serving bowls
12 crystallised white phlox flowers

Put the sugar and water in a pan and gently heat until the sugar is dissolved, stirring continually so the sugar does not stick to the pan; then boil for two minutes. Remove the pan from the heat and allow to cool. Cut the watermelon into wedges and remove the skin and the pips. Cut into rough chunks and check there are no pips left. Put into a food processor or liquidiser with syrup and lemon juice and process until you have a smooth purée. To make the granita (water ice) pour the purée into a shallow dish and

freeze for 45-60 minutes. Remove from the freezer and break up the ice crystals with a fork or electric beater. Return to the freezer. Repeat this process until you have a mass of ice crystals. Once you have the crystals, cover the container and freeze until required. Frost four glass bowls by painting the rims with the whipped egg white then standing them upside down in caster sugar. Put in the granita and garnish with the crystallised phlox.

Primula veris
COWSLIP

❖

Hardy perennial, Ht.15-20cm (6-8in). Clusters of sweetly-scented, yellow,
tubular flowers in spring. Green oval-shaped leaves.

I have been lucky enough to grow up in the West Country and have very
clear memories of walking through fields full of flowering cowslips. Due to
changes in farming practices this, alas, is no longer possible. However, if
you live on limestone or chalk, you will be able to grow them and they will
spread easily. You will be able to have cowslip wines, or eat the flowers in
salads where their flavour is sweet and evocative of the country.

HOW TO GROW

SEED

Sow the seed into prepared seed or
plug trays in early autumn. Cover the
container and winter outside as the
seeds will germinate better if they get
some frost.

DIVISION

Divide established plants in early
autumn or spring. Replant at a
distance of 15cm (6in) apart.

WHERE TO PLANT

GARDEN

Plant in semi-shade or sheltered sun,
in a moist, well-drained soil.

CONTAINER

Cowslips can be grown in containers as
long as the compost does not dry out.
Protect from the midday sun.

WHEN TO HARVEST

Pick the flowers just as they open,
when they can be preserved in wine,
sugar, syrup, and vinegar (see p138).

They also look most attractive when
crystallised (see p142).

CULINARY

To eat the flowers, you must remove
all the green bits, leaving yourself
with the complete yellow flower.
They really do taste heavenly.

TIP

This is really a word of warning. It is
prohibited in many European
countries to pick or dig up this plant if
you find it growing in the wild.

WARNING

Some *primula* flowers can cause
a form of contact dermatitis so
handle carefully.

WATERCRESS, PURSLANE
AND COWSLIP SALAD

Serves 4
2 bunches of watercress, well washed
*115g (4oz) green and gold
purslane leaves*
10-15 cowslip flowers

Salad dressing
*1 teaspoon fresh tarragon, finely
chopped*
*1 teaspoon mint (either Moroccan or
Tashkent), finely chopped*
*1 tablespoon cowslip vinegar (or white
wine vinegar)*
3 tablespoons olive oil

Roughly chop the watercress, mix
in the purslane and half of the
cowslip flowers. Make the salad
dressing by thoroughly mixing
all the ingredients together. Just
before serving, toss the salad in
the dressing and scatter over the
remaining flowers.

PANCAKES WITH COWSLIP AND ORANGE SAUCE

Serves 8
Pancakes
240g (8oz) plain flour, sifted
450ml (¾ pint) milk and water in
equal proportions
1 large egg, beaten
1 tablespoon melted butter or oil
1 tablespoon caster sugar
Pinch of salt
Oil or lard for frying

Cowslip and orange sauce
300ml (½ pint) water
175g (6oz) caster sugar
Rind from 2 unwaxed oranges
10-15 cowslip flowers, with all green
bits removed

This batter is best made in the morning and allowed to stand for the day in the refrigerator. But it will not matter if you can't.

Put the flour in a mixing bowl, make a well in the centre and gradually add the milk and water. Slowly mix together to a smooth batter, with all the flour thoroughly blended in. Add the egg, butter or oil, sugar and salt, and beat again thoroughly. The end result should be like thin cream.

To make the sauce bring the water to the boil. Add the sugar, stirring all the time to dissolve without sticking to the bottom of the pan. Add the rind of the oranges and simmer for about 10 minutes. Remove from the heat.

When ready to eat, heat enough oil or lard to coat the base of the frying pan. Stir the batter and pour a small amount into the pan, tilting the pan so a that a thin layer of batter covers the whole of the base. Let it cook until it shifts when you shake the pan; then if you dare, flip the pan to toss the pancake, or use a spatula to turn it instead. When the second side is cooked, slip the pancake onto a warmed plate and repeat till you have enough. Re-heat the sauce for a minute and pour over the pancakes. Sprinkle a few cowslip flowers over each pancake and serve.

Primula vulgaris
PRIMROSE

❖

Hardy perennial, Ht.15-20cm (6-8in). Sweetly-scented, yellow flowers with darker yellow centres in spring. Oval, wrinkled mid-green leaves.

I know that to some people it would be sacrilege to eat this herald of spring with its warm perfume. In fact, the first time I was given a salad of primrose and violets flowers, I thought likewise until I actually ate them. The flavour is the same as the scent, warm and sweet. They really do add something to a green salad on a damp, dull, spring day.

HOW TO GROW

SEED

This is not an easy plant to grow from seed. It is best to sow them as fresh as possible, in late summer into prepared seed or plug trays, and to cover and over-winter outside.

DIVISION

Divide established plants in early autumn, and replant in the garden 15cm (6in) apart.

WHERE TO PLANT

GARDEN

This native of the countryside prefers growing in hedgerows and under deciduous trees. If these conditions are not available, plant in semi-shade in a well sheltered site. The soil should be moist and rich in leaf mould.

CONTAINER

Primroses can be grown in containers but, bearing in mind their preferred habitat, position them in semi-shade and do not let the compost dry out.

TIP

This is not a tip but a word of warning. It is prohibited in many European countries to pick or dig up this plant if found growing in the wild.

WARNING

Some *primula* flowers can cause a form of contact dermatitis so handle carefully.

WHEN TO HARVEST

Pick the flowers as they open, preserve them by crystallising or by making a floral sugar or vinegar (see p138).

CULINARY

Because of the delicate flavour I prefer to eat this flower unadulterated. Remove all green bits and the stamen from the flower before eating.

PRIMROSE SALAD

Serves 4

1 round lettuce

115g (4oz) lamb's lettuce

2 tablespoons young primrose leaves, finely chopped

50g (2oz) parsley, chopped

450g (1lb) tomatoes, skinned and chopped

½ cucumber, peeled and chopped

15-20 primrose flowers

Salad dressing

3 tablespoons sunflower or olive oil

1 tablespoon primrose vinegar

(*or white wine vinegar*)
Freshly ground black pepper and salt

Wash and shake the lettuce dry, discarding the outer leaves. Add the lamb's lettuce, tomatoes, parsley, primrose leaves and cucumber and mix thoroughly. To make the salad dressing combine the oil and vinegar in a bowl, whisk thoroughly, season with pepper and salt. Pour the dressing over just before serving, toss and scatter the primrose flowers on top.

PRIMROSE AND VIOLET SALAD

Serves 4
1 iceberg lettuce (or another crisp lettuce)
15-20 primrose flowers
15-20 violet flowers (optional)

Salad dressing
3 tablespoons sunflower oil
1 tablespoon violet vinegar (or white wine vinegar)
1 tablespoon mint (Bowles or apple), chopped
Freshly ground black pepper and salt

Divide, wash, dry and then slice the iceberg lettuce. Place it on a serving plate or bowl and scatter both lots of flowers over the top. Make the salad dressing, if possible using violet vinegar, by mixing thoroughly together the oil and vinegar, adding the mint and seasoning to taste. Pour over the salad just before serving and toss.

Robinia hispida
ROSE ACACIA
❖

Hardy deciduous perennial, Ht. 1.5-2m (5-6ft). The rose-coloured flowers hang in pendent racemes and are pea-like in shape. Dark green leaves.

This is a stunningly pretty shrub, the flowers have a pea-like flavour and look most attractive when decorating puddings. *Robinia pseudoacacia*, false acacia or locust, is a deciduous, spreading tree, growing to a height of 25m (80ft). It has dense, drooping clusters of fragrant pea-like white flowers which are also edible.

HOW TO GROW
SEEDS
This shrub sometimes sets seed and it is best to sow these in early autumn as soon as they are ripe. Sow in a prepared seed tray or plug tray and winter them in a cold frame or cold greenhouse.

SUCKERS
Divide the suckers away from the main plant in autumn. Either replant in the garden if it is sheltered or pot up and winter in a cold greenhouse or cold frame.

GRAFTING
If you buy this plant from a garden centre or nursery it is worth looking for a plant that has been grafted onto *Robinia pseudoacacia*, because this will turn the shrub into an attractive small tree with darker green leaves and trusses of large pink flowers.

WHERE TO PLANT
GARDEN
Robinia has become thoroughly naturalised in Europe since it was introduced from North America. Although it is not a very long-lived shrub (tree), it will grow in any but waterlogged soil. If given a choice, it prefers poor, dry soil in a sunny position. Protect from strong winds as the branches are brittle and may snap off. Another major advantage is that this plant can withstand any sort of industrial pollution and is therefore ideally suited for growing in cities.

CONTAINER
Rose acacia will grow in containers as long as you make sure it does not get pot bound, which can happen very quickly. For a real challenge, grow a rose acacia which has been grafted onto a false acacia as a standard; it looks truly stunning and smells heavenly in summer.

WHEN TO HARVEST
Pick the complete truss of flowers just as they start to open. Preserve by crystallising (see p142) or by making a syrup (see p141).

CULINARY
To prepare the flowers for use in cooking, pick them individually from the truss, making sure no greenery or stem is attached.

TIP
Do not prune *Robinia* but just lightly trim it to keep the tree in shape. Cut out the dead wood in late summer before the leaves fall.

WARNING
DO NOT EAT the seed pods that form after flowering as they are POISONOUS.

MERINGUE NESTS WITH SUGARED ROSE ACACIA FLOWERS

Serves 4
Meringue
4 egg whites
225g (8oz) caster sugar

Filling
300ml (½ pint) whipping cream
¼ teaspoon almond essence
1 tablespoon crystallised rose acacia flowers
Preheat oven to 120°C, 250°F, gas mark 2

To make the meringue, whip the egg whites until they are very stiff, so that you can turn the bowl upside down and they will not fall out all over the floor!!! Fold in the sugar, a tablespoon at a time. Put the meringue into a forcing bag with a decorative nozzle and pipe the nests onto a baking tray lined with silicone paper. Bake in the oven for one to two hours until quite dry. Cool on a wire rack.

For the filling, whip the cream till nearly stiff and mix in the almond essence. Put the meringue nests on a serving plate, fill with the cream and decorate with the crystallised rose acacia flowers. Chill before serving.

SUMMER PUDDING WITH ROSE ACACIA FLOWERS

Serves 6
675g (1½lb) mixed fruit - blackcurrants, raspberries, loganberries, blackberries and cherries
150ml (¼ pint) water
½ sandwich loaf of white bread, thinly sliced
Granulated sugar (to taste)
1 teaspoon arrowroot, soaked in 150ml (¼ pint) fruit juice or water
1 tablespoon rose acacia flowers, separated into individual florets

Put the fruit and water in a pan, cover and simmer for four to five minutes, then strain, reserving the juice. Put the fruit in a food processor or liquidiser and blend until puréed. Add the juice to the fruit purée, mix and sweeten to taste. Cut the crusts from the bread. Line a bowl, bottom and sides with the bread cut to fit. Pour some fruit purée onto the bottom slices of the bread so that they are all well soaked, cover with one to two slices of bread on top and add more of the purée. Continue like this until the dish is full, making sure that each layer is well soaked with the fruit purée. Then make a bread lid to put on the top. Reserve a good 150ml (¼ pint) of the purée for the sauce. Put a plate and a 1kg (2lb) weight on the top of the pudding and leave overnight in the refrigerator.

To make the sauce take a small pan and add a little water to the reserved purée. Stir in the arrowroot and bring to the boil, stirring all the time over a medium heat. Pour into a bowl and cool. Turn out the pudding onto a serving dish, spoon over the sauce and decorate with the rose acacia flowers.

Rosa ssp.
ROSE
❖

Perennial, mostly hardy, deciduous or semi-evergreen shrubs and climbers. Ht. 40cm-4m (15in-12ft). Depending on species, flowers between spring and autumn in all shades of colour. The leaves are usually divided into five or seven oval leaflets.

The Chinese records of this amazing flower date back thousands of years. The Greeks, Romans and Persians all used roses for perfume and medicine. The petals have also been used in culinary delights for hundreds, if not thousands, of years. As a child, I ate rose-petal jam sandwiches when making a tea party for my animals. This was considered a delicacy in Elizabethan times. Nowadays if you do not have the time to make your own petal jam, you can buy some ready-made, based on extremely good traditional recipes.

HOW TO GROW

Growing roses successfully makes a complete book, so I am giving you only general guidelines and naming a few of my favourites. These are *Rosa* x *damascena semperflorens*, damask rose; *Rosa gallica* var. *officinalis*, the apothecary's rose, *Rosa gallica* 'Versicolor', Rosa mundi, *Rosa rugosa* which comes in pink/red, *Rosa rugosa* 'Alba' the white form and a modern rose *Rosa* 'Rosemary Harkness'.

SEED

You can grow roses from the seed in rose hips, but it does require patience. The hip should stay on the plant until fully ripe before being picked. Autumn-sown seeds usually germinate in the following spring but, as germination is usually irregular, they may lie dormant for a year, so do not give up.

CUTTINGS

Take semi-ripe cuttings in early autumn. Plant out in the spring.

WHERE TO PLANT

GARDEN

The best times for planting roses are in the spring or early autumn, in most cases in an open, sunny site in a fertile, moist but well-drained soil. Make sure you water them well during their first year. As this is a hungry plant, feed in late winter and early spring with a balanced fertiliser and in spring and summer feed every month. Do not forget to dead-head flowers to encourage the plant to go on blooming. To maintain the shape of the rose prune in early spring before the new shoots start, removing dead and damaged wood.

CONTAINER

Some of the miniature bushes look lovely grown in containers. Use a soil-based compost and feed regularly in the spring and summer with a liquid fertiliser specially formulated for roses.

WHEN TO HARVEST

If the rose smells good it will taste good. Pick the rose petals in summer from flowers just as they are opening and well before they start dropping. All rose petals are edible, and taste slightly different, but do not forget to remove the white heel from the base of the petal before eating. Preserve the petals in butter, syrup, jelly, oil, vinegar (see p138) or crystallise (see p142).

TIP

Avoid planting roses in an area where they have been grown in recent years, as problems caused by soil-borne diseases can occur.

CRABAPPLE AND ROSE PETAL JELLY

The following quantities should fill four 450g (1lb) jars

1.75kg (4lb) crabapples, washed and chopped

1.5kg (3lb) sugar (see recipe)

8 tablespoons rose petals, white heel removed

1 tablespoon rose petals for adding to jelly (large petals will need to be torn into smaller pieces)

Put the crabapples into a preserving pan and add just enough water to cover them. Bring to the boil, then simmer for about 30-40 minutes until the apples become soft and pulpy. Pour carefully into a muslin (jelly, cheesecloth) bag and drain into a large bowl for a day or overnight. Measure the juice and add 450g/1lb of sugar to every 600ml/1 pint of juice. Put into a pan and bring to the boil, adding the rose petals tied in a piece of muslin (cheesecloth). Boil for about 20 minutes until setting point is reached and then remove the cooked rose petals and any surface scum. Add the remaining (torn) rose petals and stir in. Pour into warm, sterilised glass jars and seal while still hot. Date and label.

ROSE SPONGE WITH ROSE WATER ICING AND CRYSTALLISED ROSE PETALS

Rose water can be purchased from good cookshops or chemists.

100g (4oz) butter, softened

100g (4oz) caster sugar

2 tablespoons rose petals, white heel removed

2 large eggs

100g (4oz) self-raising flour, sifted

1 teaspoon baking powder

4 drops rose water

Preheat oven to 160°C, 325°F, gas mark 3

Cream the butter and sugar together, add the rose petals, eggs, flour, baking powder and the rose water. Mix together with a wooden spoon or electric mixer until smooth and glossy. Turn into a greased 20cm (8in) sandwich tin and bake for 35-40 minutes. When well risen, just firm to the touch and shrinking away from the sides of the tin, it is cooked. Remove from the oven and turn out on to a wire rack to cool.

For the filling

100g (4oz) butter

175g (6oz) icing sugar

1-2 tablespoons rose water

Cream the butter until soft and beat in the icing sugar, a little at the time. Add enough rose water to give a fairly firm but spreading consistency.

Rose water icing

225g (8oz) icing sugar

2-4 tablespoons rose water

Sift the icing sugar into a bowl and gradually beat in sufficient rose water to give a smooth icing, thick enough to coat the back of a spoon. Use at once. Decorate the cake with crystallised rose petals.

Rosmarinus officinalis
ROSEMARY
❖

Evergreen perennial, Ht. 75cm-1.5m (30-60in). Aromatic, scented, pale blue flowers in summer. Very aromatic needle-shaped dark green leaves.

Most people know rosemary, but I am sure many do not realise that the flowers are like a miniature leaf in flavour. They are great to add to tomato and marrow dishes as well as the traditional lamb. There are many lovely different species, *Rosmarinus officinalis* 'Benenden Blue' which has dark blue flowers, *Rosmarinus officinalis* 'Majorca Pink' which has pink flowers, and *Rosmarinus officinalis* prostratus group, a prostrate rosemary, which has pale blue flowers.

ROSEMARY AND TOMATO SOUP

Serves 4

1 large onion, peeled and chopped
50g (2oz) butter
675g (1½lb) tomatoes, skinned and chopped
600ml (1 pint) vegetable or chicken stock
2 sprigs rosemary (2.5cm/1in long)
Freshly ground pepper and salt
Pinch of soft brown sugar
2 tablespoons rosemary flowers, no green bits attached

HOW TO GROW

SEED

It is possible to grow rosemary from seed of *Rosmarinus officinalis* only. It will need a bottom heat of 27-32°C (80-90°F). Sow in spring in prepared seed or plug trays. Once germinated do not over-water. Prick out into pots before planting in the garden.

CUTTINGS

Take softwood cuttings of the non-flowering new growth in spring. Take semi-hardwood cuttings of the non-flowering shoots in summer.

WHERE TO PLANT

GARDEN

Plant in a well-drained soil in a sheltered sunny position. Protect young plants in their first winter. Plant at a distance of 60-90cm (2-3ft) apart.

CONTAINER

Rosemary looks lovely in terracotta pots, especially the prostrate form. Use a well-draining compost. Keep on the dry side in winter and protect from frosts.

WHEN TO HARVEST

Pick the flowers as they open. Preserve in oil, vinegars or herb butter (see p138).

CULINARY

After removing all green bits from the flowers the whole thing is edible. I cannot resist tomato soup made with rosemary.

TIP

If you live in an area that is frost prone, never cut back the plants in autumn because the frost will damage or even kill the plant.

Peel and chop the onion. Melt the butter in a saucepan and gently sweat the onion until soft and translucent. Add the tomatoes, stir for a few minutes then pour on the heated stock. Add the two sprigs of rosemary, bring to the boil and simmer for 20 minutes, then season with salt, pepper and sugar. Put into a food processor and whizz for a few seconds. Adjust the seasoning, return to the pan and gently reheat but do not boil. Pour into the serving bowls and scatter with flowers.

STIR-FRY LAMB WITH FRENCH BEANS AND ROSEMARY

Serves 4-6

Sesame oil for stir-frying
1 large onion, peeled and sliced
650g (1½lb) lean lamb, cubed
1 teaspoon rosemary leaves, finely chopped
250g (8oz) French beans
1 tablespoon rosemary flowers, no greenery attached

Heat the oil in a wok or in a large non-stick frying pan. Add the onion and fry, stirring all the time, until it starts softening. Add the lamb and the rosemary leaves and fry, stirring continuously, for about three to four minutes, and then add the French beans, frying for a further three minutes. Toss in the rosemary flowers with the meat and beans, and arrange in a serving dish.

Serve with boiled rice and a tasty green salad.

Salvia officinalis
SAGE

❖

Perennial, Ht. 60cm (2ft). Aromatic, mauve/blue flowers in the summer.
Aromatic, green, oval-shaped, textured leaves.

Sage is an ancient plant, the aromatic leaves of which have been used to preserve food since records began. The flowers have the same flavour as the leaf, with a slight hint of sweetness which makes them an ideal accompaniment for rice, meat, duck and stir-fry dishes where an extra zing is wanted. A variety especially worth mentioning is *Salvia sclarea*, clary sage (biennial), which has most attractive flowering bracts of blue/purple/lilac and cream. These have a truly aromatic flavour and, being of pastel shades, make a lovely contrast in salads. Completely different is *Salvia elegans* 'Scarlet pineapple', pineapple sage (tender perennial), with vibrant red flowers, sweeter in flavour than the previous two mentioned; it is great with fish and salads.

HOW TO GROW

SEED

Salvia officinalis and *Salvia sclarea* are the only sages that can be grown successfully from seed. Sow in prepared seed or plug trays. A bottom heat of 15-21°C (60-70°F) helps.

CUTTINGS

Take softwood cuttings from the non-flowering new growth from all perennial sages in spring.

WHERE TO PLANT

GARDEN

Plant in a well-drained soil in a warm, dry site. The seed can be sown direct into the prepared soil in spring after the threat of frost has passed. Space the seeds 23cm (9in) apart and after germination thin to 45cm (18in) apart.

CONTAINER

Sage will grow happily in containers if you use a well-draining compost. Keep watering to the minimum in winter and protect from frost.

WHEN TO HARVEST

Pick the flowers as soon as they open. They are ideal for making floral oils or vinegar (see p142). Clary sage flowers are great in butter (see p138). Pineapple sage flowers look and taste lovely crystallised (see p142).

CULINARY

All sage flowers are edible after removing all greenery and stems. They all have varying tastes. I suggest you pick a few and try them before using them in a recipe. Go steady because the ordinary sage flowers can certainly pack a punch.

TIP

When sage is grown in containers or under protection it can become prone to red spider mite. As soon as you see the leaves beginning to mottle, check underneath with a magnifying glass and, if you can see these small red spiders, treat the plants with a liquid horticultural soap.

SAGE FLOWERS WITH MUSHROOM SALAD

Serves 4

225g (8oz) button mushrooms, cleaned
2 sage leaves, finely chopped
1 clove of garlic, finely chopped
2 shallots, finely chopped
14 sage flowers, with no green attached

For the dressing

4 tablespoons olive oil
1 tablespoon sage vinegar
½ tablespoon lemon juice
Freshly ground salt and pepper

Discard the stalks from the mushrooms and thinly slice the caps. Place in a serving bowl. Mix the sage leaves, garlic and shallots into the sliced mushrooms.

Make the dressing by mixing the oil, vinegar and lemon juice and season with the salt and pepper. Pour over the mushrooms, and then scatter the flowers over the top and lightly toss.

Serve immediately, otherwise the mushrooms will absorb the oil and the flowers will become discoloured.

CLARY SAGE FRITTERS

Makes 2
For the batter
100g (4oz) plain flour
½ teaspoon salt
2 tablespoons sunflower oil
150ml (¼ pint) warm water
1 egg white

12 clary sage flowering bracts
12 clary sage leaves
Fresh oil for deep frying
Caster sugar
1 tablespoon clary sage flowers, removed from the bracts

Make the batter well before you need it: sift the flour into a bowl, add the salt, stir in the oil and mix with enough warm water to give the consistency of fairly thick cream. Leave to stand, covered with a damp cloth or clingfilm, for one to two hours. Just before using, beat the egg white in a clean bowl until it is stiff and fold it into the batter.

Rinse the clary sage flower bracts and leaves. Gently shake them dry, then dry them on some kitchen towel. Roll a flower bract in each leaf and dip into the batter one at a time. Shake off any excess batter and drop into a large pan of oil, heated to 180°C (360°F). Do not allow them to touch each other in cooking. When done, drain on kitchen paper and place on a warmed serving dish or hot plate. When all the fritters are cooked, dredge with sugar, sprinkle on the flowers and serve straight away.

121

Sambucus nigra
COMMON ELDER
❖

Deciduous, hardy perennial, Ht. 6-7m (20-23ft). Sweetly-scented, flat heads of small star-shaped cream/white flowers in late spring and early summer. Mid-green, oval-shaped leaves in clusters of five.

Elderflowers are being used more and more in cooking. Elderflower cordial, which is readily available, is lovely on a hot summer's day. The frothy, creamy-white flowers of elder hold a special memory for me as they were the first flower fritters that I ate. They also make a delicate sorbet with lemon and combine well with gooseberries, redcurrants and raspberries. The flowers from *Sambucus nigra* 'Aurea', golden elder, can be used as you would those of *Sambucus nigra*, common elder.

HOW TO GROW
SEED
Sow ripe berries outdoors in pots 2cm (1in) deep in autumn. Cover with clingfilm or glass and winter outside. When the seedlings are well established, re-pot. Keep potted up in a cold greenhouse for the first winter and plant out in the following spring.

CUTTINGS
Take semi-hardwood cuttings in summer from the non-flowering, new growth. Winter in a cold frame or cold greenhouse. Grow in a pot for another season before planting in the garden.

WHERE TO PLANT
GARDEN
Warning: elder grows very rapidly indeed, producing new shoots 120cm (4ft) long in one season. Unless you dominate elder it will dominate you. Cut back in late autumn, then prune in early spring before the growth begins. Elder tolerates most soils and prefers a sunny position.

CONTAINER
The shorter varieties, for example *Sambucus nigra* 'Aurea', golden elder, look wonderful in a terracotta pot if placed in partial shade to stop the leaves scorching.

WHEN TO HARVEST
Pick the flowers when they are cream in colour; the flavour of those that become white is not so fresh. The flowerheads must not be bruised. If you want to dry them, they should be spread out, without touching each other, heads down on a fine nylon net over a frame. Then they will retain their colour. Alternatively you can preserve them in vinegar or oil (see p142).

CULINARY
Pick the elderflower clusters whole. Check for insects and then pick the flowers off the stalks. The stalks tend to be bitter and this can ruin sweet dishes.

TIP
If you want to eat the elderberries in autumn be sure to cook them slightly first to destroy the anthocyanide pigmentism. Otherwise you will suffer from a major upset stomach.

GOOSEBERRY AND ELDER-FLOWER CRUMBLE

Serves 6

900g (2lb) gooseberries
175g (6oz) caster sugar
2 tablespoons elderflowers, separated
into individual florets

Crumble

75g (3oz) soft brown sugar
¼ teaspoon mixed spice
225g (8oz) plain flour
75g (3oz) butter
Preheat oven to 180°C, 350°F,
gas mark 4

Make the crumble by mixing the sugar,
spice and flour together, then rub in
the butter until the mixture looks like
fine breadcrumbs. Top and tail the
gooseberries, place them in an ovenproof dish, sprinkle on the sugar with
the elderflowers and then cover with
the crumble mixture and spread out
with a fork. Put the crumble in the
oven for 30-40 minutes until the top is
golden brown.

ELDERFLOWER AND RASPBERRY TART

If you like French patisseries, this is
for you. This recipe is for a 18-20cm
(7-8in) diameter flan ring.

For rich shortcrust pastry

180g (6oz) plain flour
Pinch of salt
125g (4½oz) butter

1 rounded dessertspoon sugar
1 egg yolk
2 tablespoons water
Preheat oven to 200°C, 400°F,
gas mark 6

Filling

450g (1lb) raspberries

Glaze

4 tablespoons redcurrant jelly
1 tablespoon elderflowers

First make the pastry: sift the flour
and salt into a mixing bowl. Rub in the
butter until the mixture resembles fine
breadcrumbs and stir in the sugar. Mix
the egg yolk with the water, make a
well in the centre of the flour mixture,
pour in the egg and water, and quickly
work until you have a firm dough.
Lightly knead on a floured board
until smooth. Wrap in clingfilm and
chill for at least 30 minutes before
using. Roll out the pastry and line the
flan ring; bake blind in the oven for
about 25 minutes. Cool on a wire rack.

When cool, cover the base of the
tart with raspberries. Make the glaze
by gently heating the redcurrant jelly
until it liquefies. Do not let it boil.
Brush the fruit with the jelly, starting
in the centre and brushing outwards.
Scatter the elderflowers on top. Chill.
Decorate with more flowers if desired
before serving.

Taraxacum officinale
DANDELION

❖

Perennial, Ht. 15-23cm (6-9in). Large, brilliant yellow flowers from spring well into autumn. The leaves are oblong with a jagged edge.

If this perennial plant were elusive or difficult to grow it would be in great demand as either a salad plant, a medicinal herb or just for sheer good value with its most attractive sweet-scented flowers. But because of its invasive nature it is considered a nuisance, so it is a bonus to be able to eat it. The flowers have a sweet bitter taste, great in salads and excellent for making wine.

HOW TO GROW
SEED
This flower is better grown as an annual to prevent bitterness. Sow the seed in spring on the surface of prepared pots or plug trays. Do not use seed trays because of the developing tap root. Germination takes three to six weeks.

WHERE TO PLANT
GARDEN
I am not sure that I can honestly recommend this. However if you want a salad crop, do not sow direct into the ground but plant out from the plug trays or pots in early spring, at a distance of 30cm (12in) apart. In early summer make sure that you remove any flowerheads that are setting seed so they do not spread all around the garden.

CONTAINER
Dandelions look very pretty grown in window boxes or containers which allow enough space for their tap roots to develop. You may need to convince your neighbours by giving them a glass of dandelion wine!

WHEN TO HARVEST
Pick the flowers when you need them and use fresh. Remember they close up after picking so float them on some water and pop them into the salad at the last minute.

CULINARY
This is one plant where the whole flower can be eaten. Cut the flower off as close to the head as possible, remove the stem and all the green wispy bits (sepals) around the neck. The flowers combine well with dandelion leaves in a salad with pieces of bacon. If you are feeling brave, how about fried dandelions? Simply fry the flowers in a small amount of butter and serve. They taste wonderful and certainly add something to the traditional breakfast or can enhance an early summer green salad.

TIP
If tempted to pick dandelions from a field in the country, check with the farmer first if this is all right (you could always offer him a bottle of wine), second whether he has sprayed the field with any chemicals, and third when was the last time he slurried it!!!

DANDELION WINE

This is a true country recipe which, if put down for a year, is excellent. The flowers must be fresh and traditionally gathered on St George's Day, 23 April. It is important that the flowers should be picked in sunshine, or at midday, when they are fully opened. Do not leave the flowers sitting around; make the wine immediately.

Enough for 4 bottles
3.5 litres (6 pints) dandelion flowers, the whole head not just the petals
4.5 litres (1 gallon) water,

brought to boiling point
2 lemons
1 orange
1.4kg (3lb) sugar
1 teaspoon granulated yeast
1 teaspoon wine-making nutrient
(obtainable from chemists)
450g (1lb) raisins

Remove as much as possible of the green (stalks, etc.) from the flowers, leaving the whole flowerhead. Do not be too fussy. Put the cleaned flowers into a large bowl and pour the boiling water over the flowers. Cover (either with a lid or with clingfilm) and leave for three days, stirring once a day. On the fourth day turn the water and dandelion heads into a large pan (I use a jam-making pan) with the rind of the lemons and orange. Add the sugar and bring to the boil, stirring to make sure all the sugar dissolves. Boil for one hour, stirring from time to time. Return the mixture to the large bowl or plastic bin (not a metal container), add the juice and the pulp from the lemons and orange. Allow to stand until cool, then add the yeast and nutrient. Cover and leave for a further three days in a warm place. Then strain the liquid into fermenting bottles and divide the raisins equally amongst them. Fit traps. Leave until fermentation ceases and rack when the wine clears. If this wine is made in April it is ready for drinking by Christmas, but will improve greatly if left for a further six months.

DANDELION AND BACON SALAD
Serves 4
225g (8oz) young dandelion leaves
1 tablespoon dandelion petals
2 dandelion flowers, whole for decoration
100g (4oz) streaky bacon

Salad dressing
145ml (5fl oz) natural yoghurt
1 tablespoon sunflower oil
2 teaspoons white wine vinegar
1 teaspoon wholegrain mustard

Wash and dry the dandelion leaves and flowers. Tear the leaves into a salad bowl and add the dandelion flower petals. Make the salad dressing by mixing all the ingredients together thoroughly. Grill the bacon under a hot grill, turning once. When cooked, slice into small pieces and toss onto the dandelion leaves. Pour over the dressing, toss and decorate with the whole dandelion flowers.

Thymus vulgaris & ssp.
THYMES
❖

Perennial, Ht. creeping-30cm (12in). Tiny, tubular, mauve, pink, red, purple or white flowers in summer. Aromatic, green or variegated, small leaves.

I have lost count of how many species of thyme there are. There are over 120 identified in the *RHS Plant Finder*. They are eminently collectable and I have more than 35. The flavour of the flowers is a real complement to that of the leaves, being sweet. Do not go mad when using them as they are strongly pungent. They combine well with meats such as lamb, and also with fish and vegetable dishes especially where the taste of tomato predominates. Some varieties of thyme worth looking out for are *Thymus* x *citriodorus*, lemon-scented thyme, *Thymus longicaulis*, pine-scented thyme, *Thymus* x *citriodorus* 'Fragrantissimus', orange-scented thyme, and *Thymus camphoratus*, camphor thyme.

HOW TO GROW
SEED
In general it is better to grow thymes from cuttings or division with the exception of *Thymus vulgaris*, common thyme, and *Thymus praecox* ssp. *arcticus*, wild creeping thyme. The seed is very fine, so sow carefully on the surface of prepared seed or plug trays. Do not cover. Use a bottom heat of 15-21°C (60-70°F) to accelerate germination.

DIVISION
Creeping varieties of thyme can be propagated by division in spring. This will help the plant put on new growth and keep it from going woody in the centre.

CUTTINGS
Take softwood cuttings from the new growth in the early spring or summer.

WHERE TO PLANT
GARDEN
Plant out in the garden as soon as the soil has warmed and there is no threat of frost. If you sow seed direct into the garden, thin to approximately 20cm (8in) apart when the seedlings are large enough to handle.

CONTAINER
All thyme varieties like being grown in containers. Make sure the compost is low in nutrients and free draining; if you use a rich compost this will inhibit flowering as the energy will go into producing leaf. Equally the leaf will not taste nearly as good. When potted up, place the container in a sunny position to obtain the best flavour.

WHEN TO HARVEST
Pick the small flowers as they open and when needed. They are excellent for making oils and vinegars (see p142) for long-term preserving. My favourite is thyme flower butter (see p138), which, despite the cholesterol, is marvellous to toss vegetables in after they are cooked.

CULINARY
Thyme flowers are great with tomato-based dishes such as pasta sauces or with light cheese recipes. They are also great for jazzing up cottage cheese; don't add too many because they can be overpowering.

TIP
It is essential to trim all thymes after flowering, to promote new growth and stop the plant becoming woody.

BARBECUED TROUT WITH THYME FLOWERS

Serves 4

*4 sprigs (leaves and stem) thyme,
lemon-, orange- or pine-scented
4 trout, cleaned and gutted
Thyme flower butter
4 tablespoon thyme flowers, removed
from the stalk*

Put one sprig of thyme in each trout.
Place on the grill of a barbecue ready
for cooking. Spread some thyme
butter over the upper side of the
trout, and cook for 10 minutes. Turn
the trout and spread some more
butter on the other side. When
cooked, remove from the grill, place
on the serving plate and sprinkle
one tablespoon of flowers over each
trout. Serve with a green salad and
baked potatoes.

THYME FLOWER AND AUBERGINE DIP

Serves 6-8

*1 large aubergine, peeled
2 tablespoons olive oil
450g (1lb) natural yoghurt
1 tablespoon thyme leaves, finely
chopped
2 cloves of garlic, crushed
2 tablespoons orange juice
Salt and freshly ground black pepper
1 tablespoon thyme flowers*

Cut the aubergine into small dice and
place in a colander. Sprinkle with salt
and leave for 30 minutes. During this
time the aubergine should start to sweat.
Rinse under the cold water tap and pat
dry with kitchen towel.

Heat the olive oil in a frying pan
and cook the aubergine for 8-10
minutes, turning occasionally until it is
soft and golden brown. Remove from
the heat and put into a food processor.
Blend with the yoghurt, thyme leaves,
garlic and orange juice until you have
a smooth purée. Season with salt and
pepper to taste. Pour into a serving
bowl and stir in half the thyme
flowers. Use the remaining flowers for
garnish. Cover and chill in the
refrigerator until required. This dip
goes well with hot, toasted pitta bread.

Trifolium pratense
RED CLOVER
❖

Hardy perennial, Ht. 10-40cm (4-16in). The tiny, red, pea-shaped flowers grow in clusters to form a round/oval shape all summer. The large oval leaflets are frequently marked with a whiteish band.

Have you ever lain on the lawn in summer and watched the bumble bees with their long tongues feasting on a clover, or walked through an old-fashioned meadow where the clover grows knee-high, picking off the clover heads and sucking the sweet nectar from the flowers? If so you will understand that these flowers fall naturally into the 'Good enough to eat' category. They are excellent in salads, both green and sweet, and with vegetable dishes. There are many varieties of clover, all of which are edible. *Trifolium repens*, white or Dutch clover (a perennial) is a spreading variety, *Trifolium incarnatum*, crimson clover (annual) has hairy stems and a deep crimson flower, the cluster shape being much more oval than other species. This variety is grown as an animal fodder crop and can also now be seen along roadsides, although it is not originally a native to Britain.

TIP
This plant has been used medicinally since ancient times, as it is a soporific.

HOW TO GROW
SEED
Red clover can be grown from seed if you prepare the seed first by rubbing it between two sheets of sandpaper; this is called scarification and will help germination. Sow the seed on the surface of a prepared seed or plug tray, press in and DO NOT cover.

WHERE TO PLANT
GARDEN
Trifolium pratense is the true wild form of red clover. Beware of the agricultural varieties which are far more common and which, if allowed, can take over the garden. Red clover prefers a free-draining soil with a bit of moisture, although it will withstand moderately dry conditions.

CONTAINER
If you want to grow a mixed wild flower container, then red clover is a great choice, mixed with *Viola tricolor*, wild pansy (heartsease) and *Taraxacum officinale*, dandelion.

WHEN TO HARVEST
Pick the complete flowerhead before the colour fades. It does not preserve well so is best to use it fresh.

CULINARY
It is worth picking the florets off individually to get the best flavour. Make sure that they have no green whatsoever attached to them. Scatter them over a salad or vegetable dish just before serving.

ARTICHOKE HEARTS WITH CLOVER FLOWERS AND CUCUMBER SAUCE

Serves 4
60g (2oz) butter
45g (1½oz) plain flour
450ml (¾ pint) milk
150ml (¼ pint) cream (or crème fraîche)
A drop or two of Tabasco sauce
1 tablespoon dill, chopped
1 cucumber, diced, with or without the skin (I usually leave the skin on)
Freshly ground salt and black pepper
4 artichoke hearts, fresh or tinned, cut in half
1 crisp lettuce, shredded
6 clover heads, divided into individual florets with green bits removed

Melt the butter in a saucepan, add the flour, stirring until it is absorbed, and cook for two minutes. Gradually stir in the milk and the cream, the Tabasco and the dill. Mix thoroughly and add the diced cucumber, simmering for a few minutes. Check for seasoning, adding salt and freshly ground pepper to taste. Then add the artichoke hearts. Arrange lettuce leaves on each plate and place a spoonful of the mixture in the centre, making sure there is an artichoke heart in each portion. Scatter with clover florets and serve.

GREEN AND YELLOW COURGETTES WITH RED CLOVER FLOWERS

Serves 4

2 green courgettes
2 yellow courgettes
1 dessertspoon olive oil
1 clove of garlic, crushed
Salt and freshly ground black pepper
2 tablespoons clover flowers,
separated into florets

Wash the courgettes and top and tail them. Put them into a large pan of boiling water and boil for four minutes. Remove from the heat, drain and slice. In a clean pan heat the olive oil, add the garlic and the courgettes, and toss gently, seasoning to taste. Arrange in a serving dish, scatter with the clover florets and serve.

Tropaeolum majus
NASTURTIUM
❖

Hardy annual, Ht. average 30cm (12in). Red, orange and yellow flowers from summer to early autumn. Round, mid-green leaves.

The custom of eating the petals of this jolly annual originates from the Orient. The flowers have a slightly peppery scent and a strong pepper flavour, which goes well with cream cheese, salads, vegetables and potatoes. There are many great varities of nasturtium to look out for. *Tropaelomums majus* 'Alaska' has variegated cream and white leaves with red, orange and yellow flowers. *Tropaeolum majus* 'Empress of India' has mid-green leaves with lovely dark, red flowers. Both look great in green salads.

HOW TO GROW
SEED
The seeds are large and easy to handle. Sow in early spring for flowering in early summer. Sow under protection directly into prepared pots or plug trays and cover lightly with compost. Alternatively sow the seeds individually direct into the garden 20cm (8in) apart, when all threat of frost has gone and the soil has started to warm.

WHERE TO PLANT
GARDEN
Nasturtiums prefer a well-drained poor soil in full sun or a small amount of shade. If the soil is rich the plant will put on leaf growth at the expense of the flowers.

CONTAINER
This flower is excellent in pots, tubs, hanging baskets or window boxes. I cannot stress enough, however, that you should not use a high-nutrient potting compost as this will inhibit the flowering.

WHEN TO HARVEST
Pick the flowers when they first open. As they do noy dry, use them fresh.

CULINARY
Because of their peppery flavour nasturtiums complement salads, especially when served with a vinaigrette; they also enhance cream cheese, potatoes or crème fraîche.

TIP
Pests can be a problem to nasturtiums, especially aphids (black fly) and caterpillars of the cabbage white family. If the infestation is light, then wash off with a hose, but if more prolific use a horticultural soap following manufacturer's instructions.

'EMPRESS OF INDIA' WITH NEW POTATOES

This recipe came about because I had some cold, left-over, new potatoes. You can use any nasturtiums, but the deep red of 'Empress of India' makes a good contrast with the creamy colour of the potatoes.

Serves 4
250g (8oz) cooked, cold, new potatoes
6 'Empress of India' nasturtium flowers
6 'Empress of India' nasturtium leaves
(young ones)
2 whole flowers for decoration

French dressing

1 tablespoon white wine vinegar

3 tablespoons olive oil

Pinch of brown sugar

1 teaspoon Dijon mustard

Salt and freshly ground black pepper

Make the French dressing by mixing together the vinegar, oil, sugar and mustard and seasoning to taste. Remove the petals from the flowers and add to the salad dressing. Cut up the new potatoes, chop the nasturtium leaves and combine with the potatoes in a serving bowl. Shortly before serving, pour over the dressing and toss well. Delicately place the whole nasturtium flowers as decoration.

NASTURTIUM SALAD

Serves 4

6 nasturtium flowers, petals only

6 young nasturtium 'Alaska' leaves

2 tablespoons salad rocket leaves

1 crisp lettuce, washed and divided

5 whole nasturtium flowers

French dressing

1 tablespoon white wine vinegar

3 tablespoons olive oil

1 clove of garlic, crushed

1 teaspoon Dijon mustard

Mix the nasturtium petals, the 'Alaska' leaves, the salad rocket and the lettuce in a serving bowl. Make the French dressing by mixing all the ingredients together thoroughly. Pour over the salad and toss. This looks sensational with the whole nasturtium flowers arranged on top.

131

Valeriana officinalis
VALERIAN
❖

Hardy perennial, Ht. 1-1.2m (3-4ft). Sweetly-scented clusters of white/pink flowers in the summer. Mid-green, deeply toothed leaves.

The flowers, which grow in clusters by streams or in wetlands, have a lovely, warm, musky scent which wafts through the air on a summer's day. This is totally different from the roots which positively stink when exposed to the air. The flowers of valerian have a warm, aromatic taste and go well with fruit dishes especially those with a pungent flavour, passion fruit, nectarines and bananas. Please do not confuse *Valeriana officinalis* with *Centhranthus rubra*, red valerian, (shown below right) which grows in walls, on rocks and along coastal regions and is not edible.

HOW TO GROW

SEED
Sow the seeds in spring in prepared plug or seed trays. Press into the compost, DO NOT cover the seeds with compost or perlite. When germinated and large enough to handle plant at a distance of 60cm (24in) apart.

WHERE TO PLANT

GARDEN
Plant valerian where the roots can remain cool, for example near water. It will grow well in most soils, in sun or shade. Cats love the scent of valerian roots so choose where to plant with care otherwise they will dig it up for you before you want it moved and then invite their friends to join in.

CONTAINER
Valerian is a bit large for growing in containers and also the roots can get a bit too hot in the summer. So I don't recommend it.

WHEN TO HARVEST
Pick the flowers as they open. It is easier to remove the complete cluster. They do not preserve very well so use them fresh. Make sure you remove any green from each flower before eating.

CULINARY
Valerian's flowers have a musky flavour and go well with fruit. The first time I ate these flowers was when I was barbecuing bananas whole in their skins. When ready, they were split and some valerian flowers were scattered down the middle. They were quite delicious. The recipe opposite is an adaptation of that basic recipe.

TIP
When valerian is planted near vegetables it boosts their growth by stimulating earthworm activity.

VALERIAN FLOWERS, KIWI FRUIT AND PASSION FRUIT SALAD

Serves 4
2 passion fruit
3 tablespoons apple juice
3 kiwi fruit, peeled and sliced
1 tablespoon valerian flowers

Halve the passion fruits and scoop the pulp into a serving bowl. Add the apple juice and kiwi. Mix gently and sprinkle the valerian flowers on top.

BAKED BANANAS WITH VALERIAN FLOWERS

Serves 4-6
8 bananas, peeled
8g (¼oz) butter
1 tablespoon brown sugar
1 tablespoon sherry

2 tablespoons valerian flowers
Preheat oven to 180°C, 350°F,
gas mark 4

Slice the bananas and place in an ovenproof dish, slice the butter and put it over the top. Sprinkle over the sugar and pour on the tablespoon of sherry. Sprinkle half of the flowers over the bananas, cover and put in the oven for 15-20 minutes until the bananas have become soft. Remove from the oven and scatter the remaining tablespoon of valerian flowers over the bananas. Serve with crème fraîche or double cream.

Viola odorata
SWEET VIOLET

❖

Hardy perennial, Ht. 7cm (3in). Sweetly-scented, mauve, white, pink or purple flowers in the early spring. Green, heart-shaped leaves.

As a child I remember eating Parma violet (a hybrid of sweet violet) chocolates. On the top was a whole crystallised violet which I always saved until last. The taste and the scent are totally memorable, the flavour is described as perfumed which I think is apt because they do taste as they smell. The *Viola riviniana*, common dog violet, and the *Viola reichenbachiana*, wood violet, are also edible, but they do not have that perfumed flavour or scent, more of a plain sweet flavour. However they do look just as attractive added to green or potato salads.

HOW TO GROW

SEED
Sow the small seed into prepared seed or plug trays using a soil-based compost. Cover with compost and water in well. Cover with glass or clingfilm and winter outside so that the seeds are exposed to frost. This will aid germination (stratification).

DIVISION
Violets set runners; remove these in late spring and replant into a prepared site in the garden 30cm (12in) apart.

WHERE TO PLANT

GARDEN
Violets grow naturally in the lee of hedges so when planting them in your garden give them a bit of shade. They prefer a moderately heavy soil, rich in humus so if your soil is light add some well-rotted manure.

CONTAINER
Violets will grow happily in containers as long as they have some shade. In winter do not protect the plants because violets need a period of cold to thrive.

WHEN TO HARVEST
Pick the flowers just as they open for using fresh or preserving in oil, butter, vinegar or crystallising (see p138).

CULINARY
As violets have, in my mind, always been associated with chocolate here is a recipe for 'Petits Pots de Crème' from my grandmother, Ruth Lowinsky's cook book *Food for Pleasure*. 'Take three pieces of eating chocolate, one pint of milk, four yolks of eggs. Melt the chocolate, throw in the milk and eggs and two table-spoonfuls of sugar. Mix well together, pour into ramekins and cook for 25 minutes in a tin with water. Enough for six people.' For modern-day use:

VIOLET CHOCOLATE POTS

Serves 6
600ml (1 pint) milk
4 egg yolks
2 tablespoons caster sugar
100g (4oz) plain chocolate
150ml (¼ pint) whipped cream
6 crystallised violets
Preheat oven to 180°C, 350°F, gas mark 4

Follow my grandmother's instructions up to the point 'pour into the ramekins'. Place the filled pots in water in a bain-marie or in a deep ovenproof dish on a baking sheet covered with buttered paper. Cook in the oven for 12-15 minutes until just set. Take out and chill in a refrigerator. Serve with a dollop of whipped cream in the centre and a crystallised violet in the centre of that.

SWEET VIOLET SORBET

Serves 4

24 sweet violet flowers
75g (3oz) caster sugar
300ml (½ pint) water
Juice of 1 large lemon
1 egg white
8 sweet violet flowers for decoration

Make sure the violets are clean and, if necessary, wash and pat dry using a kitchen towel. Put the sugar and water in a saucepan and boil, stirring, until the sugar has dissolved. Add the 24 violets, cover the pan and turn off the heat allowing the violets to infuse for 20 minutes. If the flavour is too weak, gently bring back to the boil and then immediately remove from the heat and allow to stand for a further five minutes. Pour the syrup into a firm container, add the lemon juice, stir and leave to cool. It is personal preference at this point whether or not you remove the infused violets. They do look a bit bedraggled and my son kindly said they looked like dead flies, so I leave the decision to you. Put the syrup into the freezer for about one hour until semi-frozen. Beat the egg white in a bowl until it is stiff and dry. Fold this into the semi-frozen violet syrup. Return to the freezer until frozen, about another hour. Spoon into four glass dishes, decorate each with two fresh or crystallised violets.

Viola tricolor
HEARTSEASE

❖

Hardy perennial, often grown as an annual, Ht. 15-30cm (6-12in). Small tricolour pansy-shaped flowers from spring until autumn. Green, deeply-lobed leaves.

The flowers vary a great deal in colour, being either purple, yellow or white, but most commonly there is a combination of all these colours in each blossom. In the language of flowers this has bequeathed the saying 'Think of me', which is said to have been derived from the French for pansy, *pensée*. They taste of a mixture of sweet, soft violet (which is not surprising as they are related to *Viola odorata*, sweet violet) and gentle lettuce. In the following section I outline only how to use heartsease but this could easily apply to any *Viola* x *wittrockiana*, garden pansy. Both flowers combine well not only in green salads and other flower salads but also equally well in fruit salads, looking most attractive with pears, peaches or melons.

TIP
An infusion of heartsease flowers has traditionally been prescribed for a broken heart.

HOW TO GROW

SEED
Sow seeds under protection in autumn in prepared seed or plug trays. Do not cover. Harden off in the spring and plant out in the garden or in containers.

WHERE TO PLANT

GARDEN
Heartsease will grow in any soil in partial shade or sun. Plant at a distance of 15cm (6in) apart. If you wish to sow direct into the ground press the seed into the soil, but do not cover.

CONTAINER
These small flowers are ideal for growing in containers, from hanging baskets through to terracotta pots. Use the flowers as much as possible

and, to keep the plant flowering longer, pick off the dead flowers as they wither.

WHEN TO HARVEST
Pick the flowers when fully open from spring right through until late autumn. Normally use fresh although they will, at a push, dry (see p146).

CULINARY
As I have mentioned, this flower is very mild in flavour. The plus point is that the whole flower can be eaten, stamens and all, so it is a bonus to have a fully edible attractive garnish adding an extra something to all forms of salads. Equally the gentle flavour is a plus when you do not want the flavour of your dish masked or hidden.

PEARS WITH HEARTSEASE IN RED WINE

Serves 6
145g (5oz) granulated sugar
150 ml (¼ pint) red wine
A few strips of lemon rind
Small stick of cinnamon
150 ml (¼ pint) water
6 ripe dessert pears, peeled but retaining the eye and stalk
1 teaspoon arrowroot
3-4 tablespoons whole heartsease flowers

Make a syrup by putting the sugar, wine, lemon rind, cinnamon stick and water into a large saucepan and slowly, stirring from time to time, bringing to the boil. Simmer for one minute. Place the pears in the syrup, cover the pan and poach for about 20-30 minutes until tender and cooked completely through. Remove the pears and strain the syrup. Mix the arrowroot with a little water and add to the syrup. Once added return to the heat and keep stirring until the liquid becomes clear. Arrange the pears in a serving dish, spoon over the syrup and toss the heartsease over the top. Place in refrigerator. Serve cold.

'PRINCE HENRY' IN A CANTELOUPE

There are many edible violas, *Viola* 'Prince Henry' is another variety with blue purple flowers.

Serves 2
1 canteloupe melon
6 'Prince Henry' heartsease flowers
2 teaspoons Cointreau

Cut the canteloupe in half and remove all the pips, saving the juice. Mix the juice with the Cointreau and divide between the two melon halves. Float three 'Prince Henry' flowers in each half and serve chilled.

PRESERVING FLOWERS

Preserving flowers for culinary use is not as difficult as one thinks, for in the majority of cases it is not the flower or scent that you need to preserve but the flavour. In general, plants flower once a season, so it is important to be able to capture that moment so prolonging their availability. The traditional techniques of drying and freezing do not readily adapt to preserving the flavour of flowers and I therefore prefer using butter, oil, jelly and syrups in which I have found that the floral flavours combine well. Equally, where one wants to preserve a whole flower, I recommend crystallising as an ideal method.

FLORAL PRESERVES

With all the following recipes I have provided general information. There are many different variations on a theme which can include combinations of different flowers. If you require more specific information please refer to the individual flower chapters.

FLORAL BUTTER

Floral butter can be substituted in any recipe that uses butter. For example, rose petal butter is lovely in a Victorian cake mix, spread directly onto bread or buns or when used to make a white sauce. Bergamot butter used in making a béchamel is superb with chicken or fish. When making carrot soup, try sweating the carrots in thyme flower butter before adding the stock. The possibilities are endless.

*8 tablespoons prepared flower petals
250g (½lb) unsalted (or low salt)
butter, softened*

Finely chop the flower petals. Put the softened butter into a bowl, add the chopped petals and mix well. Cover the bowl and let the mixture rest at room temperature for a few hours. Put into a container with a sealing lid and place in the refrigerator and leave for a few days to allow the flavour to develop. This butter will keep in the refrigerator for about two weeks or alternatively you could freeze it and then it will keep for three months. If you are freezing the butter do not forget to label it.

FLORAL SUGAR

Floral sugar can be used in any culinary recipe instead of regular sugar. The flavour is not as strong as the butter. The best floral sugars are made from flowers with a sweet, definite scent such as lavender, rose, violets, pinks, mint and citrus flowers. Meringues made with floral sugar are quite something else.

FLORAL SUGAR

Serves 4
*350g (¾lb) granulated or caster
sugar*
*8-16 tablespoons chopped flower
petals*

Put the sugar and flowers into a
food processor or liquidiser and
blend well. Put the floral sugar into
a glass jar, cover well and let it stand
for a week. After this time, sift the
sugar and flowers through a
medium sieve and put into an
airtight container. If you wish you
can layer it, flowers, sugar, flowers,
sugar as in the photograph of
lavender sugar on p139. This looks
wonderful and is inspirational, but
is not very practical, because when
you use the sugar for cooking you
could land up having a large flower
in the middle of your meringues!!
Having said that, the top layer of
sugar tastes marvellous.

FLORAL SYRUP

Floral syrup is very useful and ideal
when making fruit salads, sorbets,
or any pudding needing an aromatic
syrup base.

300ml (½ pint) water
*450g (1lb) granulated or
caster sugar*
*8-16 tablespoons flower petals or
6 whole flowers e.g. elder,
meadowsweet, sweet cicely, etc.*

Bring the water to the boil in a
saucepan, turn down the heat and
add the sugar, stirring all the time.
When the sugar has dissolved, add
the flower petals, stirring from time
to time, and gently boil the mixture
until it turns into a syrup. This can
take up to eight minutes. Strain the
syrup through a fine sieve or some
muslin (cheesecloth) if you want
absolutely no flower bits left. Pour
the cleaned syrup into a clean glass
jar, allow to cool, seal well and store
in the refrigerator for up to two weeks.

FLORAL JELLY

If you have a lot of apples this is a
great way of preserving the flavour of
flowers to use through the winter. If
you belong to a church or you have
children at school, then pots of this
preserve will always be welcome.

**The following quantities should fill
four 450g (1lb) jam jars**
*1.75 kg(4lb) cooking apples, washed,
chopped and cored*
1.75 litres (3 pints) water
1kg (2lb) sugar
*6 large complete flowers (elder,
meadowsweet, sweet cicely)*
*8-16 tablespoons of flowers or a
mixture of flowers, dependent on taste*
4 tablespoons lemon juice

Put the apples into a large pan
with a lid, add the water and bring
to the boil, then simmer until the
apples become soft and pulpy,

about 20-30 minutes depending on
the variety of apple.

Pour carefully into a muslin bag
(jelly or cheesecloth) and leave for a
day or overnight to drain into a large
bowl. When finished, measure the
juice and add 450g (1lb) of sugar to
every 600ml (1 pint) of juice. Put
into a pan and bring to the boil,
adding the flowers tied in a piece of
muslin (cheesecloth). Leave one
tablespoon of flowers aside if you
would like to decorate the jelly with
the flowers. Boil for about 20 minutes
until setting point is reached.
At this point remove the flowers in the
muslin and spoon off the surface
scum. Stir in the lemon juice and
one tablespoon of petals if required
and pour into warmed clean glass
jars. Seal when cool, date and label.

141

FLORAL OILS

Everyone who knows me knows that I love making herb oils. I think this is a marvellous way of preserving the flavour of the herb or flower to use in cooking or in the making of salad dressings. The gentle oil flavour suits some of the more strongly flavoured flowers like basil, bergamot, thyme and sage.

1 jam jar filled with flowers either single species or mixed
Olive oil to cover. I prefer olive oil (not extra virgin) but vegetable oil can be substituted as long as it does not have a strong flavour of its own.

Place the petals or whole flowers in a clean jam jar (preferably with a screw top), cover with oil. It is important

that the oil covers all the flowers and that no flowers are peeking out, otherwise they will go mouldy. Place the jar on a sunny windowsill and for the next month shake the jar when you remember or when you need to shake something else. After a month strain through a clean coffee filter (this is ideal for straining free-flowing liquids). Pour the strained oil into a pretty bottle and add a complete flower or some petals to decorate.

FLORAL VINEGAR

Like floral oils this is easy to make and adds an extra dimension to cooking, great for different sauces or marinades. The other advantage of floral vinegars is that, because one heats the vinegar with the flower, quite often the white wine vinegar changes colour. For example nasturtium flowers turn the vinegar orange/yellow, red rose petals a deep pink, chive flowers a pale pinkish lavender.

450ml (¾ pint) white wine vinegar
4-8 tablespoons flower petals

When cooking any vinegar never use an aluminium pan because the acid will react with the pan; use stainless steel or a glass saucepan. Gently heat the vinegar, NEVER allow it to boil. Put the petals/flowers in a jar with a lid (not metal) and pour the hot vinegar over, allowing an air space of approximate 1.5cm (½in) from

the top. Allow the vinegar to cool to room temperature before putting on the top. Leave for three to four weeks, then strain and pour into a new jar or attractive bottle. Add a fresh flower, petals or sprig as decoration. This can equally be made with cold vinegar; simply set the bottles of flowers in vinegar on a sunny windowsill with their tops tightly closed. Shake the bottles each day as you pass and after two or three weeks test the vinegar for flavour and fragrance. If they are satisfactory, strain and return the vinegar to a clean bottle with a single flower or some petals as decoration. Label the bottle.

CRYSTALLISED FLOWERS

There are a number of methods for crystallising flowers, the most common being to dip them in beaten egg-white with sugar with or without alcohol, but the one I prefer uses gum arabic and rose water. This will preserve the flowers for a few months if kept in an airtight container. However this method does take time, so be patient.

1 tablespoon rose water (This can be bought from the dispensary of any large pharmacist. Inform them you wish to use the rose water for cookery and they will make it up using tap water, which is better than purified water which has had its salts removed. The salts are necessary to control any bacteria.)

1 teaspoon gum arabic (This can be bought from pharmacies or stores selling cake-making and icing accessories.)
Icing sugar or caster sugar
2 thin fine clean paint brushes
Greaseproof paper or baking parchment
Wire cake rack
Airtight containers

When crystallising flowers it is essential to be well prepared because the fresher you crystallise the flowers the better the end result. So prepare the gum arabic solution first by pouring one tablespoon of rose water into a small jar (which has a close-fitting top and a wide enough neck to be able to pop flowers in and retrieve them), and then adding one teaspoon of powdered gum arabic. Replace the top and shake the bottle until the powder has dissolved, about one to two minutes. Do not be tempted to put the powder into the jar first and then add the rose water because it is then incredibly difficult to make the powder dissolve fully.

Pick the flowers in late morning choosing perfect specimens. Dip first in water to remove any insects or dust, then dry gently on kitchen towel. Cut away the stems and any green parts, also the white heels from the petals of roses and clove pinks. Immerse the flowers completely in the gum arabic solution, by dropping them one at a time into the bottle. With one of the paint

brushes (artist's brushes are best), retrieve the flowers from the jar and lay them on paper which has been covered with sugar. Sprinkle more sugar over the flowers and use the second brush to remove any sugar which has formed lumps in the hearts of the flowers. Place the now well-sugared flowers to dry on a layer of greaseproof paper on a cake rack in a cool oven with the door ajar. When they are hard to the touch, store them in layers between greaseproof paper in airtight jars or rigid containers.

FREEZING FLOWERS

This is a popular way to preserve and store herbs because it's quick and easy, however it is only suitable for a few flowers and even for these it is better when they are in bud. An ideal flower to freeze is the day lily.

Pick and, if necessary, rinse in cold water and pat dry. Put the flowers individually on a tray (not touching) and place in the coldest part of the freezer. Once frozen gently put a few flowers into a plastic bag and label.

then put the bags into a container so they do not get damaged with the day to day use of the freezer. There is no need to thaw the flowers before use, simply add to the dishes as required.

Another method of freezing which suits small or individual flowers is to use ice cubes. These floral cubes can be added to drinks, fruit salads and other deserts. For example, borage looks very attractive when frozen individually in ice cubes (see p145 for illustration).

DRYING FLOWERS

I am not a great advocate of drying flowers for use in cooking because the drying, however fast you do it, causes the flowers to lose their vibrant colours and also their unique textures. However for those of you who want to try, here are some basic points.

The place chosen for drying must be dark, warm, dry and well ventilated, such as:
1. The oven at a low temperature setting with the door ajar,
2. The domestic airing cupboard,
3. An oven plate warming compartment,
4. A spare room with the curtains shut and the door open,
5. Old-fashioned attic immediately under the roof (provided it does not get too hot).

The temperature should be maintained slightly below body temperature 21-33°C (70-90°F)

If using the oven, place flowers on a piece of brown paper with holes punched in and check regularly that the flowers are not overheating.

With other methods of drying, the flowers should be spread in a single layer on trays or slatted wooden racks covered with muslin or netting. The trays or frames are then placed in the drying areas so that they have air circulating beneath as well as on top. The shallow wooden boxes with the raised corners used by the greengrocer for tomatoes and other vegetables are ideal as they can be stacked on top of each other and still allow for ventilation.

The flowers need to be turned over by hand several times during the first two days.

An alternative method is to tie them in small bundles of eight to ten flowering stems and then hang them on coat hangers in an airy dark room, until they are dry. Do not pack the stems too tightly together as air needs to circulate through and around the bunches.

The length of drying time will vary. The determining factor is the state of the plant material. If flowers are stored before drying is complete, moisture will be reabsorbed from the atmosphere and the material will soon deteriorate. The flower petals should be both brittle and crisp and break easily into small pieces but should not be reduced to a powder when touched.

EDIBLE GARDENS

The following four conceptual edible themes can be copied exactly as the design or easily adapted to suit your space and tastes. An important factor when creating an edible garden is accessibility; you will need to be able to get at the plants. So all the gardens have some form of path or a shape that enables the plants to be reached.

FORMAL GARDEN

In designing this I took an idea from my first garden which was a small town-house garden. Although the space was confined, I wanted a seat. So I put as much of the ground as possible down to garden and constructed a path from the back door to the seat, which I then backed with sunflowers. When these grew taller than my fence and turned to face the sun, they gave my neighbours nearly as much pleasure as they gave me. The remaining plants that I have chosen will give colour and shape to the garden. There are also enough annuals to be able to ring the changes as your palette develops.

Alcea rosea hollyhocks
Angelica archangelica angelica
Borago officinalis borage
Calendula officinalis marigolds
Chamaemelum nobile chamomile
Cichorium intybus chicory
Dianthus ssp. pinks
Eruca vesicaria ssp. *sativa* salad rocket
Filipendula ulmaria meadowsweet
Foeniculum vulgare fennel
Helianthus annuus sunflowers
Hesperis matronalis sweet rocket
Hyssopus officinalis hyssop
Lonicera caprifolium honeysuckle
Monarda didyma bergamot
Myrrhis odorata sweet cicely
Oenothera biennis evening primrose
Pelargonium scented geraniums
Perilla frutescens var.*crispa* shiso
Primula vulgaris primroses
Robina hispida rose acacia
Rosa gallica 'Versicolor', Rosa Mundi,
Rosa 'Albertine' climbing rose
Rosmarinus officinalis rosemary
Salvia officinalis sage
Sambucus nigra elder
Thymus vulgaris thyme
Tropaeolum majus nasturtiums
Viola odorata violets

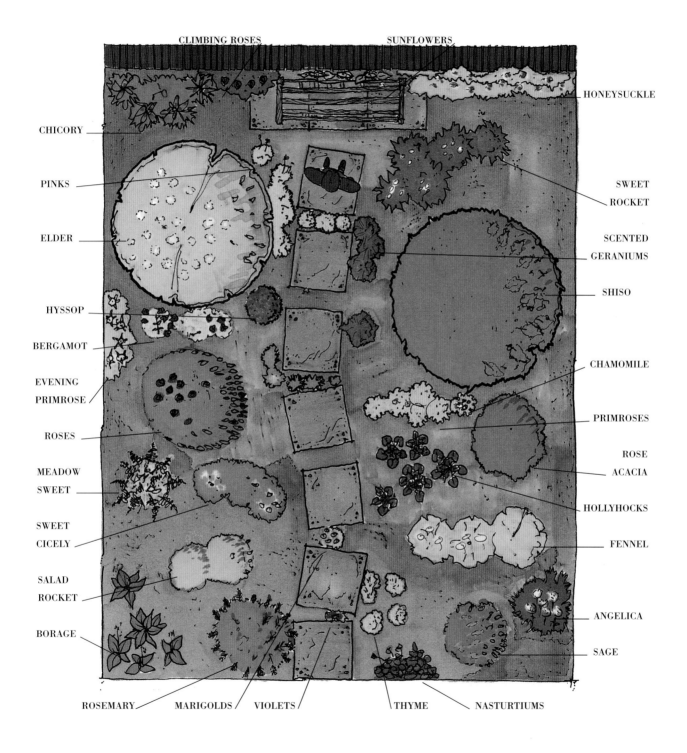

CLIMBING ROSES

SUNFLOWERS

HONEYSUCKLE

CHICORY

PINKS

ELDER

HYSSOP

BERGAMOT

EVENING
PRIMROSE

ROSES

MEADOW
SWEET

SWEET
CICELY

SALAD
ROCKET

BORAGE

ROSEMARY

MARIGOLDS

VIOLETS

THYME

NASTURTIUMS

SWEET
ROCKET

SCENTED
GERANIUMS

SHISO

CHAMOMILE

PRIMROSES

ROSE
ACACIA

HOLLYHOCKS

FENNEL

ANGELICA

SAGE

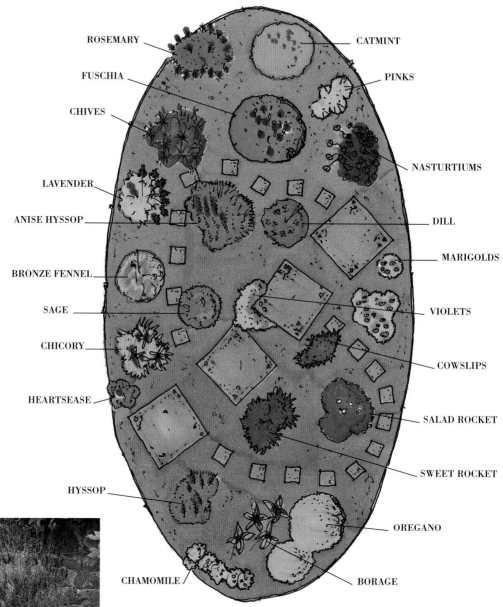

ROSEMARY

CATMINT

FUSCHIA

PINKS

CHIVES

NASTURTIUMS

LAVENDER

ANISE HYSSOP

DILL

MARIGOLDS

BRONZE FENNEL

SAGE

VIOLETS

CHICORY

COWSLIPS

HEARTSEASE

SALAD ROCKET

SWEET ROCKET

HYSSOP

OREGANO

CHAMOMILE

BORAGE

INFORMAL GARDEN

The oval shape allows accessibility to plants; however it is always a good idea to add some extra stepping stones so that you are able to reach the plants in the middle with the greatest of ease. When you let the plants mature you will have a subtle blend of colours which, as well as being lovely to eat, will be pleasing to the eye. This garden has the bias to blue which will make it very tranquil. The odd splash of gold from the marigolds and cowslips and the white from the chamomile add a sparkle to the blue/mauve sea.

Agastache foeniculum Anise hyssop
Allium schoenoprasum chives
Anethum graveolens dill
Borago officinalis borage
Calendula officinalis marigolds
Chamaemelum nobile chamomile
Cichorium intybus chicory
Dianthus ssp. pinks
Eruca vesicaria ssp. *sativa* salad rocket
Foeniculum vulgare 'Purpureum' bronze fennel
Fuchsia ssp. fuchsia
Hesperis matronalis sweet rocket
Hyssopus officinalis hyssop
Lavandula angustifolia lavender
Nepeta x *faassenii* catmint
Origanum vulgare oregano
Primula veris cowslips
Rosmarinus officinalis rosemary
Salvia officinalis sage
Tropaeolum majus nasturtiums
Viola odorata violets
Viola tricolor heartsease

DINNER PARTY GARDEN

I enjoyed doing this design. I imagined putting the dinner table in the gap between the three beds and serving the meal outside using the flowers from the different gardens. The great thing about this garden is that each bed is a garden in itself so if you do not have much space, you could plant up just one.

FIRST COURSE

Coriandrum sativum coriander
Hemerocallis ssp. day lily
Perilla frutescens var. *crispa rubra* shiso purple
Tropaeolum majus 'Empress of India' Nasturtium 'Empress of India'

MAIN COURSE

Chrysanthemum coronarium chopsuey

Cucurbita pepo var. green bush F1 courgette
Monarda fistulosa bergamot
Oenothera biennis evening primrose
Thymus vulgaris thyme

PUDDING

Angelica archangelica angelica
Fuchsia ssp. fuchsia
Phlox paniculata 'Album' white phlox
Viola odorata violets
Viola tricolor heartsease

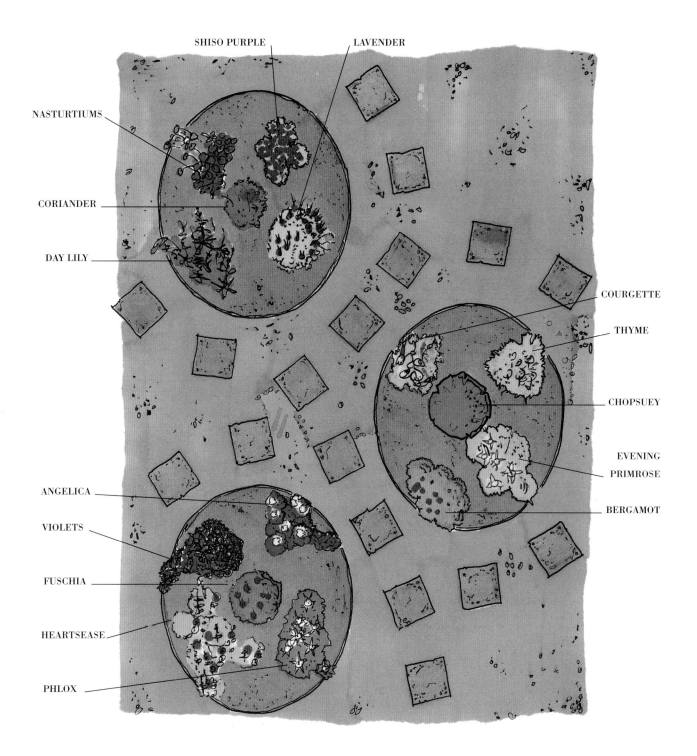

SHISO PURPLE

LAVENDER

NASTURTIUMS

CORIANDER

DAY LILY

COURGETTE

THYME

CHOPSUEY

EVENING
PRIMROSE

ANGELICA

VIOLETS

BERGAMOT

FUSCHIA

HEARTSEASE

PHLOX

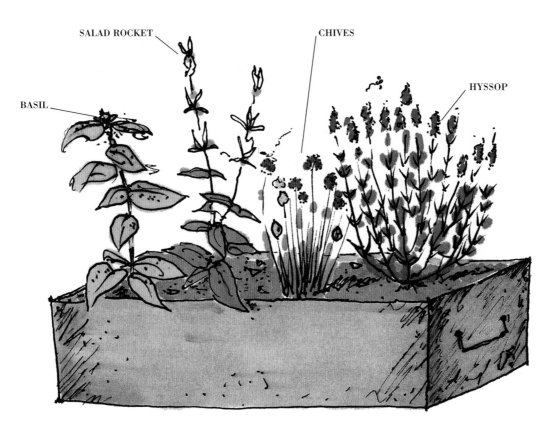

SALAD ROCKET

CHIVES

HYSSOP

BASIL

EDIBLE WINDOW BOX

When planting in a container the secret to keeping the plants happy is a good potting compost. I recommend a bark-peat-grit mix of compost which I have found suits the majority of plants. The other tip is to water regularly throughout the growing season. Also, as the container will inhibit the plants' natural growth, make sure you feed regularly throughout the spring and summer,

especially if you require lots of flower. In this box I have put:

Allium schoenoprasum chives
Eruca vesicaria ssp. *sativa* salad rocket
Hyssopus officinalis hyssop
Ocimum basilicum basil

There are no restrictions on what you can put in the container; just check that they do not grow too tall and topple over on a windy day, or that they will not invade other plants'

growing space, mint for example is guilty of this. If you want a real splash of colour, how about:

Calendula officinalis marigolds
Helianthus 'Big Smile' dwarf sunflower
Tropaeolum majus 'Empress of India'
Nasturtium 'Empress of India'

In the entry for each plant I have said whether or not it is suitable for growing in containers. This will enable you to make up your own boxes without too much difficulty.

GENERAL GUIDE TO EATING FLOWERS

As with all plants, make sure you know whether or not the plant and flower are edible before you eat or cook them. This book identifies the most common flowers that can be eaten. In addition a list of the more common plants that must NOT be eaten is provided opposite. However, beware neither list is exhaustive, therefore please err on the side of caution for any plants that you are not 100 per cent sure about.

Check that no sprays or chemicals have been used on the flowers especially when buying plants or flowers from a garden centre or florists. Remember that produce that are not normally grown as a food product will not have the strict chemical controls applied. Equally, do not pick flowers for eating close to the road sides because they will have been polluted by traffic and dust. In all cases it is preferable to pick flowers grown by yourself, where you can be sure that organic methods have been used.

If when out walking in the country, you are tempted to pick flowers in the wild, be warned it is against the law in Great Britain. This applies to cowslips, primroses and violets, to name a few. However, if you see a field covered in dandelions and are tempted to make some dandelion wine (see p124) I am sure if you asked the farmer first and offered him a bottle of wine he would be most willing for you to pick the flower heads off, unless of course he is going to make some wine himself.

Some flowers are only added to food for decoration and are not edible, for example sweet peas, daffodils and buttercups. So be cautious and check the list opposite. If you are at all unsure the best rule of thumb is do not eat it. If you suffer from hay fever or asthma, be careful. Eat a minute amount of petal first, making sure there is no pollen attached, to check on your reaction.

You should pick the flowers on a dry day when they are in bud or newly opened. The best time of day for picking flowers is before midday when the dew has dried and the sun has not become too hot to draw out the essential oils. Flowers in full bloom are past their best in fragrance and flavour. Gently wash in cold water to remove any insects or dust and gently pat dry on kitchen paper. Always remove any green parts (stalks, sepals) from the flowers and the pistils and stamen before eating because the pollen may cause an allergic reaction in susceptible individuals. Only the petals of some flowers are edible, for example, roses, pinks, marigolds, chrysanthemums and lavenders (for more information check the individual flower descriptions). When using just the petals, separate them from the rest of the flower just before using to keep wilting to a minimum. Cut away the white heels from the base of rose and clove pink petals because these will taste bitter.

When tasting a flower, especially for the first time, start by eating only the petals. Take it slowly and you may be delighted by the flavour. However, if you do not like it do not despair, try another such as a mint flower which will freshen your mouth. Do not go mad and pig out on your border. Eat small amounts to start with, not every dish suits a flower!!

INEDIBLE FLOWERS

A useful list of FLOWERS AND PLANTS THAT ARE TOXIC and/or POISONOUS. So give them a wide berth. This is certainly NOT all, but the ones you are most likely to come across. So I stress ... know what you are eating before putting it in your mouth ... or the mouths of others.

BOTANICAL NAME	COMMON NAME	BOTANICAL NAME	COMMON NAME
Aconitum napellus	Monkshood, Aconite, Wolfsbane	*Hedera helix*	Ivy
		Helleborus foetidus	Stinking Hellebore
Acorus calamus	Sweet Flag, Calamus, Myrtle Flag	*Helleborus niger*	Christmas/Lenten Rose
		Helleborus viridis	Green Hellebore
Actaea spicata	Baneberry	*Hyacinthus orientalis*	Hyacinth
Aethusa cynapium	Fool's parsley	*Hyoscyamus niger*	Henbane
Agrostemma githago	Corncockle	*Iris* ssp.	Iris all species
Anemone ssp.	Anemone all species	*Lathyrus* ssp.	Sweet pea all species
Aquilegia vulgaris	Columbine	*Ligustrum vulgare*	Privet
Arnica montana	Arnica, Leopard's Bane	*Mercurialis perennis*	Dog's mercury
Arum maculatum	Lords and Ladies	*Narcissus* ssp.	Daffodil all species
Atropa belladonna	Deadly nightshade	*Oenanthe crocata*	Water Dropwort
Bryonia dioica	White, Red Bryony, English Mandrake	*Ornithogalum umbellatum*	Star of Bethlehem
		Prunus laurocerasus	Laurel, Cherry laurel
Buxus ssp.	Box all species	*Ranunculus* ssp.	Buttercup, & Celandine, all species
Caltha palustris	Marsh Marigold		
Colchicum autumnale	Meadow Saffron, Autumn Crocus	*Rhododendron azalea* ssp.	Azalea all species
Conium maculatum	Hemlock	*Solanum dulcamara*	Wood nightshade, Bittersweet
Convallaria majalis	Lily of the Valley		
Digitalis purpurea	Foxglove	*Solanum tuberosum*	Potato
Euonymus europaeus	Spindle tree and other species of Euonymus	*Vinca* ssp.	Periwinkle all species
		Viscum album	Mistletoe
Euphorbia ssp.	All spurges	*Wisteria* ssp.	Wisteria all species

INDEX